Grammar Practice

Grade 7

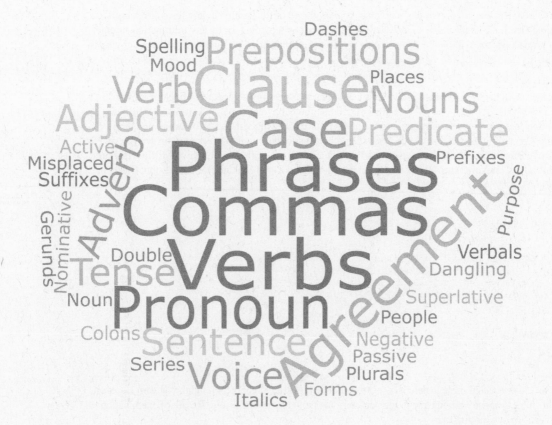

Table of Contents

MODULE 1: THE SENTENCE
SENTENCE SENSE

1a A *sentence* is a group of words that expresses a complete thought. A sentence begins with a capital letter and ends with a period, a question mark, or an exclamation point.

EXAMPLES   The writing lab has several new computers.
Please be on time for play rehearsal.
Have you read the module on the Civil War?
Stop the car now!

1b A *declarative sentence* makes a statement. It is always followed by a period.

EXAMPLES   Shanti was elected class president two years in a row.
Here are two more suggestions.

1c An *imperative sentence* gives a command or makes a request. It is usually followed by a period. A strong command is followed by an exclamation point.

The subject of a command or a request is always *you,* but *you* doesn't usually appear in the sentence. When *you* is absent, it is called the **understood subject.** *You* is the understood subject even when the person is addressed by name.

EXAMPLES   [You] Please shut the window.
[You] Watch out!
Rosaria, [you] please read the first two sentences aloud.

1d An interrogative sentence asks a question. It is followed by a question mark.

EXAMPLES   How did you know my name?
Do you live in Canada?

1e An exclamatory sentence shows excitement or expresses strong feeling. It is followed by an exclamation point.

EXAMPLES   What an exciting soccer game that was!
I can't believe we are finally at the cabin!

EXERCISE 1   Identifying Sentences

On the line before each item, write *S* if the group of words is a sentence or *NS* if it is not a sentence. If it is a sentence, add correct punctuation.

EX. __NS__ Whenever she rides her mountain bike

__S__ Alana wears her helmet whenever she rides her mountain bike.

_____ 1. Before the music began to play
_____ 2. Did Brad send Danielle a bouquet of yellow roses
_____ 3. Listening to the distant sound of thunder and seeing lightning crack across the nighttime sky
_____ 4. There is a way out of the tunnel
_____ 5. There wasn't much left to eat by the time Malcolm arrived
_____ 6. Dr. García uses all the latest equipment in her dental practice
_____ 7. Walking to the party
_____ 8. Tyrone sat on the beach because he had broken his ankle
_____ 9. Imagine what could happen in the future
_____ 10. Where did I put my library card

EXERCISE 2   Classifying and Punctuating Sentences

Classify each of the following sentences by writing *D* for declarative, *IMP* for imperative, *INT* for interrogative, or *E* for exclamatory on the line before the sentence. Then add the correct punctuation.

EX. __E__ How loud that music is!

_____ 1. Every year, the island loses sand to the shifting tides and shrinks by an inch or two
_____ 2. What a frightening experience that was
_____ 3. Hang up your coat in the front closet
_____ 4. I can't believe how close to us that dolphin swam
_____ 5. Were you able to answer all the questions on that test

RUN-ON SENTENCES

1f   A *run-on sentence* is two complete sentences punctuated as one sentence.

In a run-on, the thoughts run into each other. The reader cannot tell where one idea ends and another begins.

RUN-ON   Latanya is a finalist in the tennis tournament, let's watch the match tomorrow.
CORRECT   Latanya is a finalist in the tennis tournament. Let's watch the match tomorrow.
RUN-ON   Latanya plays basketball she's also on the tennis team.
CORRECT   Latanya plays basketball, **and** she's also on the tennis team.

To spot run-ons, read your writing aloud. A natural, distinct pause in your voice usually marks the end of one thought and the beginning of another. If you pause at a place where you don't have any end punctuation, you may have found a run-on sentence.

To revise run-on sentences, use one of the following methods.

(1) Make two sentences.

RUN-ON   Charles Drew was a doctor and a teacher he taught at Howard University.
CORRECT   Charles Drew was a doctor and a teacher. **He** taught at Howard University.

(2) Use a comma and a coordinating conjunction (*and, but, or, so, because, since*).

RUN-ON   Drew taught classes, he performed operations.
CORRECT   Drew taught classes, **and** he performed operations.

FYI   A comma marks a brief pause in a sentence, but it does not show the end of a sentence. Always use a conjunction with a comma between complete ideas.

RUN-ON   Drew was a pioneer in blood research, he experimented with plasma.
CORRECT   Drew was a pioneer in blood research, **and** he experimented with plasma.

EXERCISE 3   Identifying and Revising Run-ons

Rewrite each run-on sentence correctly. You can rewrite it as two sentences or use a comma and a coordinating conjunction.

EX.   Tony Garulo has a farm he raises miniature horses there.
<u>Tony Garulo has a farm. He raises miniature horses there.</u>

1. The farm is in Pennsylvania it is near the city of Gettysburg.

_____

2. Garulo went to Argentina he learned about Falabella horses there.

_____

3. They look just like full-sized horses they are the size of dogs.

_____

4. They are very tame they seem to enjoy performing.

_____

5. Visitors can watch the horses jump, these animals also dance and pull tiny wagons.

_____

EXERCISE 4   Revising to Correct Run-Ons

Rewrite the paragraph below to correct the run-on sentences.

     Our class went on a spring trip to Baltimore, Maryland, it was really fun. In the morning, we strolled along the Inner Harbor and looked at all the sailboats, we saw a tropical rain forest and a coral reef at the National Aquarium in Baltimore. Later, we visited Fort McHenry, the flag waving over this fort gave Francis Scott Key the idea to write "The Star-Spangled Banner." Finally, we toured the USS *Constellation*, one of the first U.S. warships, it was built in 1797.

_____

_____

_____

_____

_____

_____

_____

_____

MODULE 1: THE SENTENCE

THE SUBJECT

1g   The *subject* tells whom or what the sentence is about.

To find the subject of a sentence, ask *who* or *what* is doing something or *whom* or *what* is being talked about. The subject may come at the beginning, the middle, or the end of a sentence.

EXAMPLES   On his trip to the Amazon rain forest, **Mr. Bergeron** took hundreds of photographs. [*Who* took photographs? *Mr. Bergeron* did.]

Hanging from the thick tree branch was a **hairy sloth**. [*What* was hanging from the tree branch? A *hairy sloth* was.]

The **rain forest** is the habitat of many interesting animals. [*What* is being talked about? The *rain forest* is.]

1h   The *complete subject* consists of all the words needed to tell *whom* or *what* a sentence is about. The *simple subject* is the main word or words in the complete subject.

EXAMPLE	**That spiny little creature** is a hedgehog.
COMPLETE SUBJECT	**That spiny little creature**
SIMPLE SUBJECT	**creature**
EXAMPLE	Does **Groundhog Day in the United States** fall on February 2?
COMPLETE SUBJECT	**Groundhog Day in the United States**
SIMPLE SUBJECT	**Groundhog Day**

NOTE   In this module, the term *subject* means the simple subject unless it is defined otherwise.

EXERCISE 5   Identifying Subjects

Underline the simple subject in each of the following sentences.

EX. The <u>rain forest</u> supports a tremendous diversity of life.

1. Many scientists are now studying rain forest plants.
2. The National Cancer Institute knows of over 2,000 rain forest plants with cancer-fighting properties.

3. In her report, Jenna explained the effect of the rain forest on the weather.
4. The rain forest in the Amazon region influences the rainfall there.
5. "El Yunque" is the name of a rain forest in Puerto Rico.
6. With its fierce winds, Hurricane Hugo practically eliminated the Puerto Rican parrot from El Yunque.
7. Roaming the rain forests of New Guinea are huge, ferocious birds called cassowaries.
8. Standing almost as tall as a human, cassowaries have wings but can't fly.
9. The female cassowary lays four to eight green eggs on the forest floor.
10. Do people know enough about ways to preserve the world's rain forests?

EXERCISE 6   Identifying Complete Subjects and Simple Subjects

Underline the complete subject in each sentence. Then draw a second line under the simple subject.

EX. <u>Our history <u>teacher</u></u> told us about the Shona people.

1. The people of this culture lived in southern Africa many years ago.
2. The buildings of their capital city still stand today.
3. The capital, called Great Zimbabwe, lies near the Sabi River.
4. More than ten thousand people may have lived in the capital city.
5. Every year, fascinated tourists come to this home of one of the great cultures of the ancient world.

THE PREDICATE

1i   The *predicate* consists of all the words that are not part of the complete subject.

Like the subject, the predicate may be found anywhere in a sentence.

EXAMPLES   The Lincoln Memorial **is a national monument**.
                High above all the other buildings in Washington, D.C., stands the
                    Washington Monument.
                Throughout the city, we **saw historic sites**.

1j   The *verb,* or *simple predicate* is the main word or phrase doing the action in the complete predicate.

        EXAMPLE   The author **autographed copies of his latest book**.
     PREDICATE   **autographed copies of his latest book**
         (VERB)   **autographed**

A *verb phrase* has a main verb and one or more helping verbs. Helping verbs include *will, can, do, should, would, could,* and forms of the verbs *be* and *have.*

NOTE   The words *not* and *never* are adverbs, not verbs. They are never part of a verb or verb phrase.

EXERCISE 7   Identifying Predicates

Underline the complete predicate in each of the following sentences.

    EX.   <u>On July 4, 1986</u>, Americans <u>celebrated the birthday of the Statue of Liberty</u>.

1. Two million people gathered along the shore of New York Harbor.
2. The occasion was the hundredth birthday of Lady Liberty.
3. For the big event, workers repaired the statue.
4. The repairs cost more than 69 million dollars.
5. The Statue of Liberty was ready for her birthday party.
6. She had new elevators, a new torch, and a repaired crown.
7. At the celebration, spectators saw a dazzling display of fireworks.
8. Forty thousand fireworks soared into the sky over the harbor.
9. From the enormous crowd of people came a loud chorus of cheers and applause.
10. This was one of the largest displays of fireworks in the history of the United States.

EXERCISE 8   Identifying Complete Predicates and Verbs

Underline the complete predicate in each sentence. Then write the verb or verb phrase on the line following the sentence.

EX.   You <u>should have brought pictures of your vacation</u>.

should have brought
_____

1.   A local actor and comedian writes funny stories about her childhood.
_____

2.   The library will be closed on Fridays during the summer.
_____

3.   The boys want pizza and salad for supper.
_____

4.   I can never remember how to fold an origami crane.
_____

5.   Put the dirty dishes in the sink.
_____

COMPOUND SUBJECTS AND COMPOUND VERBS

1k A *compound subject* consists of two or more subjects that have the same verb. The subjects are usually connected by *and* or *or.*

EXAMPLES The **bear** and the **badger** hibernate in the winter. [*Bear* and *badger* are both subjects of the verb *hibernate.* The two parts of the subject are connected by *and.*]

Freda, Thomas, or his **sister** will babysit for the Grants. [*Freda, Thomas,* and *sister* are all subjects of the verb phrase *will babysit.* The three parts of the subject are connected by *or.*]

1l A *compound verb* consists of two or more connected verbs that have the same subject. A connecting word—usually *and, or,* or *but*—is used to join the verbs.

EXAMPLES Kim **trained** hard and then **worked** as a camp counselor. [Both verbs, *trained* and *worked,* have the same subject, *Kim.*]

Namir **may set** the table, **serve** the meal, or **wash** the dishes. [*Namir* is the subject of the verbs *may set, serve,* and *wash.*]

Sometimes the subject of a sentence is difficult to locate. In such cases, find the verb first and then ask yourself *whom* or *what* the verb describes.

EXAMPLES In English class, we are reading poetry. [The verb phrase is *are reading. Who* are reading? *We* are reading. *We* is the subject of the sentence.]

In the bowl were ripe fruit and cheese sticks. [*Were* is the verb. *What* were in the bowl? The answer is *fruit* and *sticks. Fruit* and *sticks* are the subjects.]

EXERCISE 9   Identifying Compound Subjects

Circle the verb and underline the compound subject in each sentence.

EX.   <u>Nutrition</u> and <u>health</u> (are) interesting topics.

1. Apples and oranges are healthy choices for a snack.
2. Vitamin C and dietary fiber are found in apples.
3. However, oranges and the juice of oranges contain five times as much vitamin C.
4. Iron and vitamins are plentiful in whole wheat bread.
5. White eggs and brown eggs are equally nutritious.

EXERCISE 10   Identifying Compound Verbs

In each sentence, circle the verbs or verb phrases that make up the compound verb and underline the subject, which may be single or compound.

EX.   Some <u>people</u> (can operate) huge machines but (will) not (touch) a computer.

1. The sun gives light and provides warmth.
2. Baby penguins stand on their parents' feet and cuddle.
3. John bought tickets but never arrived for the play.
4. Dodo birds and dinosaurs once existed but now are extinct.
5. In late autumn, the leaves on the oak tree turn bright red and fall to the ground.
6. Staple or clip the pages of your report together.
7. The *Titanic* hit an iceberg and sank.
8. The math problems looked hard but were really very simple.
9. Will Tamika or Jaylon drive us to the movie and take us home later?
10. Magda read the book and then wrote a review of it for the school website.

MODULE 1: THE SENTENCE
MODULE REVIEW

A. Identifying Sentences by Purpose

On the line before each sentence, identify it by writing *D* for declarative, *IMP* for imperative, *INT* for interrogative, or *E* for exclamatory. Then add the correct punctuation mark.

EX. <u>INT</u> Would you rather see a movie about baseball or watch a baseball game?

_____ 1. Deval, use that remote to turn on the television
_____ 2. There are so many great movies to choose from
_____ 3. Would you like to pick a movie for us to watch
_____ 4. I can make some popcorn while you decide
_____ 5. Don't touch that hot bag yet

B. Identifying Complete Subjects and Complete Predicates

Underline the complete subjects once and the complete predicates twice in the following sentences.

EX. <u>The entire population of the city</u> <u>welcomed the winning team back home</u>.

1. The baseball team had never won a championship in the history of our school.
2. During the season, the players and coaches worked hard.
3. Their dedication to the game was obvious.
4. Among their greatest achievements was perfect attendance by each player.
5. People in this town may never again feel such pride and joy.

C. Identifying Simple Subjects and Verbs

In each sentence, underline the simple subject once and the verb or verb phrase twice.

EX. <u>Dorothea Dix</u> <u>became</u> a schoolteacher at the age of fourteen.

1. This amazing woman also wrote children's books.
2. In 1841, she visited a jail in Massachusetts.
3. The jail housed not only criminals but also people with mental illness.
4. The Massachusetts schoolteacher was horrified.
5. Because of Dix's work, states built proper hospitals for people with mental health problems.

D.   Using Compound Subjects and Compound Verbs in Writing

Imagine that you live in the year 2300. You have been on a long journey into space. On the lines below, write notes for a log that tells about your experience. Write your notes in sentence form. Include and label at least five compound subjects and five compound verbs in your notes. These are some of the questions you might answer:

1. What did you see on your journey?
2. Did you make any stops? If so, where?
3. What was the most unusual experience you had on your journey?
4. What was the most amusing thing that occurred on the journey?
5. What was the most frightening thing that happened on your journey?

                                                        comp. verb

EX.   June 14, 2300—After 25 days in space, we <u>saw</u> and <u>photographed</u> an amazing meteor collision.

_____

_____

_____

_____

_____

_____

_____

_____

_____

_____

_____

_____

_____

_____

_____

_____

_____

MODULE 2: PARTS OF SPEECH
NOUNS

Words in the English language are classified into groups according to the jobs they perform in sentences. These groups are called *the eight parts of speech*: *nouns*, *pronouns*, *adjectives*, *verbs*, *adverbs*, *prepositions*, *conjunctions*, and *interjections*.

2a   A *noun* is a word that names a person, place, thing, or idea.

Persons	Yo-Yo Ma, children, choir
Places	Utah, desert, restaurant, island
Things	llama, money, plants, Nobel Prize
Ideas	truth, justice, love, freedom

2b   A *proper noun* is a specific name for a particular person, place, thing, or idea. It always begins with a capital letter. A *common noun* is a general name for a kind of person, place, thing, or idea. It is not capitalized.

Proper Nouns	Common Nouns
Michelangelo	painter
South America	continent
USA Today	newspaper
Jason Reynolds	author

Notice that some nouns are made up of more than one word. Such nouns are called ***compound nouns***. As the following examples show, the parts of a compound noun may be joined or written separately.

EXAMPLES   tablecloth   Hollywood   Abraham Lincoln
                   brother-in-law   high school   Labor Day

2c   A *concrete noun* names a person, place, or thing that can be perceived by one or more of the senses (sight, hearing, taste, touch, and smell). An *abstract noun* names an idea, a feeling, a quality, or a characteristic.

Concrete Nouns	sea, drumbeat, yogurt, deer, roses
Abstract Nouns	loyalty, curiosity, health, grace, sweetness

EXERCISE 1   Identifying and Classifying Nouns

Underline each noun in the sentences below. Then, on the line before each sentence, write *C* if the noun is concrete or *A* if it is abstract. If there is more than one noun in a sentence, separate your answers with a semicolon.

EX. __C; C__   The jellyfish is an unusual animal.

_____ 1. I feel joy each time I walk on the beach.
_____ 2. The Milky Way contains several hundred billion stars.
_____ 3. Harriet thought an eternity had passed.
_____ 4. Lois Weber was among the pioneers in making movies.
_____ 5. In ancient Greece, winning athletes were awarded a leafy crown.

EXERCISE 2   Revising Sentences by Using Proper Nouns

Revise each sentence by substituting a proper noun for each common noun. You may need to change some of the other words in the sentence. You may also make up proper names.

EX.   My parrot sounds just like my uncle. _____
         Paco sounds just like Uncle Mort. _____

1. The president traveled to his hometown. _____

    _____

2. That novel was written by my best friend. _____

    _____

3. A story about a large building was in the newspaper. _____

    _____

4. This popular actress stars in a remake of an animated movie. _____

    _____

5. My cousin moved to a city in a faraway country. _____

    _____

PRONOUNS

2d   A *pronoun* is a word used in place of a noun or more than one noun.

EXAMPLE   Gather the chickens and put the chickens in the henhouse.
Gather the chickens and put **them** in the henhouse.

Pronouns can be singular or plural, depending on the noun or nouns they replace.

Singular	I, me, my, mine, you, your, yours, he, him, his, she, her, hers, it, its, myself, yourself, himself, herself, itself, this, that, everybody, someone
Plural	we, us, our, ours, you, your, yours, they, them, their, theirs, ourselves, yourselves, themselves, these, those

An *antecedent* is the word that a pronoun stands for (or refers to).

EXAMPLE   Because the **senator** thought the crowd looked bored, **she** finished **her** speech
early. [*Senator* is the noun that *she* and *her* refer to.]

Sometimes, an antecedent is not stated.

EXAMPLES   **I** hoped Kameron would enjoy our party.
Francis wondered **who** was at the door.

NOTE   The pronouns *they*, *them*, *their*, and *theirs* are usually plural, but they can sometimes
be used informally to refer to a single person. They may also refer to a person who
uses these pronouns.

EXERCISE 3   Identifying Pronouns and Antecedents

Underline all pronouns in the following sentences. Put two lines under the antecedent of each
pronoun. Write *none* above any pronoun that has no antecedent.

EX.   Leo said that he would run the business.

1. Startled by its own shadow, the pony slipped out of its halter.
2. Mr. Chisholm spent most of his vacation at the beach.
3. Please buy the red flowers, because they are the most colorful.

4. Because he was so tired from chopping wood, the lumberjack took his lunch break early.
5. Rafael said, "I am ready to go home now."
6. "For some reason, I thought New Hampshire was in the other direction," said Jaime.
7. Abuelo won the race in his age group.
8. "Adam, you should clean your room thoroughly before you go out," said Mom.
9. Jason said, "Alejandro, do you want to ride with me?"
10. I asked Andrés if he had done his homework.

EXERCISE 4   Identifying Nouns and Pronouns

Rewrite each sentence, replacing the underlined words or phrases with pronouns. [Note: If necessary, rearrange some of the words.]

EX.   Leonardo da Vinci was a great painter, but <u>Leonardo da Vinci</u> was also an inventor.
       <u>Leonardo da Vinci was a great painter, but he was also an inventor.</u>

1. Leonardo da Vinci painted <u>Leonardo da Vinci's</u> masterpiece the *Mona Lisa* in the early 1500s. _____

2. Some people disagree about the real name of the painting *Mona Lisa*—<u>the real name of the painting</u> could be *La Gioconda*. _____

3. Lisa del Giocondo was the model for the painting, and <u>Lisa del Giocondo</u> was an Italian noblewoman. _____

4. Because Mona Lisa's smile is unusual, <u>Mona Lisa's smile</u> has caused many arguments. _____

5. Because many painters wanted to paint like da Vinci, <u>many painters</u> copied <u>da Vinci's</u> masterpiece. _____

ADJECTIVES

2e   An *adjective* is a word that modifies a noun or a pronoun.

To *modify* a word means to describe the word or to make its meaning more definite. An adjective modifies a noun or a pronoun by telling *what kind, which one, how much,* or *how many.*

What Kind?	Which One *or* Ones?	How Many *or* How Much?
long weekend	*last* year	*thirty* days
fast skates	*his* toys	*no* wheels
cheerful nurse	*our* friend	*ninety* people

NOTE   A possessive form of a pronoun (such as *our*, *your*, *his*, and *their*) modifies a noun by answering the question *Whose?* Because a possessive pronoun functions as an adjective, it may be labeled as both a pronoun and an adjective.

Sometimes an adjective comes after the word that it modifies.

EXAMPLE   The play was **funny**. [The adjective *funny* modifies *play*.]

When a noun modifies another noun or a pronoun, it is considered an adjective.

Nouns	Nouns Used as Adjectives
school	*school* calendar
summer	*summer* storm
city	*city* lights
turkey	*turkey* dinner

NOTE   The words *a, an,* and *the* are called **articles**. *A* and *an* are called **indefinite articles** because they refer to someone or something in general. *The* is called a **definite article** because it refers to someone or something in particular.

EXERCISE 5   Identifying Adjectives

Underline the adjectives in the sentences below, and draw two lines under the noun or pronoun each adjective modifies. Do not include the articles *a, an,* and *the.*

EX.   Many students rode on the purple bus.

1. Most tornadoes occur on hot, humid days.
2. When we toured the city, we saw shiny new skyscrapers next to old historical buildings.
3. Summer temperatures lasted for only two months.
4. She saw many stars in the clear sky.
5. The moon weighs 81 billion tons.

EXERCISE 6   Using Nouns as Adjectives

Pick four words from the list below. For each word, write two sentences on the lines provided. Use each word first as a noun, then as an adjective.

EX. annual   The annuals in our garden are daisies.
              The annual picnic always attracts a large crowd.

dress	wood	committee	boat	Lincoln	scratch
blue	Texas	seafood	speech	cat	flower

1. _____

   _____

2. _____

   _____

3. _____

   _____

4. _____

   _____

DEMONSTRATIVE AND PROPER ADJECTIVES

2f *This, that, these*, and *those* can be used both as adjectives and as pronouns. When they modify a noun, they are called *demonstrative adjectives*. When they are used alone, they are called *demonstrative pronouns*.

Demonstrative Adjectives	How long did it take you to come to **this** conclusion about **that** subject? **These** pearls are superior to **those** pearls.
Demonstrative Pronouns	**This** came from Tanzania, and **that** came from Zambia. **These** belong with **those**.

2g A proper adjective is formed from a proper noun.

Proper Nouns	Proper Adjectives
Poland	*Polish* hat
Fourth of July	*Fourth of July* cookout
Galileo	*Galilean* method
Asia	*Asian* countries

EXERCISE 7   Identifying Demonstrative Adjectives and Pronouns

In each sentence, underline demonstrative adjectives once and underline demonstrative pronouns twice.

EX. This is a story about those bears.

1. The weather has been very hot in this part of the state.
2. That chair beside the table was made by my grandfather.
3. Fruit is my favorite food during this time of year.
4. Those who wish to go to the beach should follow this path.
5. These basketball sneakers were made by a local company.

EXERCISE 8   Identifying Common and Proper Adjectives

In the following paragraph, underline the common adjectives once and underline the proper adjectives twice. Do not include the articles *a, an,* and *the*.

EX.   <u>Denim</u> jeans originated in an <u>Italian</u> town.

[1] There, a cotton cloth similar to denim was used to make work clothes. [2] The town, Genoa, was known to French weavers as Genes. [3] An immigrant tailor, Levi Strauss, came to San Francisco during the 1850s and sold heavy canvas for making tents. [4] He realized that the gold miners quickly wore out their trousers from the hard work. [5] Strauss made many overalls for the miners from his heavy-duty fabric. [6] After a few years, he replaced this canvas material with a softer fabric, denim. [7] Strauss borrowed an idea from a Russian Jewish tailor to strengthen the pockets by adding copper rivets at the pocket seams. [8] He used blue fabric so that stains would not show. [9] The San Francisco denim became quite famous. [10] In 1935, these practical trousers became popular when a fashion magazine ran an advertisement for them.

MODULE 2: PARTS OF SPEECH
MODULE REVIEW

A. Identifying Nouns, Pronouns, and Adjectives

Identify each italicized word in the sentences below by writing *N* for a noun, *P* for a pronoun, or *A* for an adjective on the lines before the sentences. Separate your answers with a semicolon.

EX. <u>N; P or A</u>   *Laverne* spent many hours practicing *her* speech.

_____ 1. The construction *workers* stopped for a *lunch* break.
_____ 2. If history repeats *itself, we* are in for one big surprise.
_____ 3. When *you* are thirsty, *heat* becomes less bearable.
_____ 4. After the celebration, *Jiro* walked to the *train* station.
_____ 5. In swimming, the *front* crawl used to be called the *Australian* crawl.
_____ 6. *Tasmania* is *part* of Australia.
_____ 7. The Tasmanian devil has *black* fur with white *patches*.
_____ 8. Did *Picasso* paint *this* picture or sculpt that monument?
_____ 9. Did *you* buy a *British* novel?
_____ 10. Even though *he* is reading that speech, the ideas in it are from *Maggie*.

B. Identifying Pronouns and Antecedents

In the sentences below, underline each pronoun once, and double underline its antecedent. [Note: A sentence may have more than one pronoun.]

EX.   The <u>director</u> said that <u>she</u> would promote the play with a series of social media posts.

1. Adriana, are you going fishing?
2. Louis Armstrong, known to his fans as "Satchmo," had a brilliant smile.
3. We, the performers, have decided to override the director's decision.
4. Ask Wenona if she brought her sandwiches for the picnic.
5. "I built that castle myself," said the small boy.

C. Identifying Adjectives

In the following paragraph, underline the adjectives once, and underline the words that they modify twice. Do not include *a, an,* and *the.*

EX.   The <u>popular</u> <u>author</u> James Herriot wrote <u>several</u> <u>books</u>.

[1] One excellent book was made into a popular television series. [2] The setting for Herriot's powerful stories is beautiful Yorkshire, England, where the grassy hills make a rich background for several memorable characters. [3] All the major characters are not humans, though. [4] Because Herriot was a real-life veterinarian, most of these outstanding stories feature animals. [5] In many ways, Herriot's books are unforgettable tours through the small, rural towns of the northern part of England.

VERBS

3a A *verb* is a word that expresses an action or a state of being.

EXAMPLES The rabbit **scampered** into the bushes.
Lionel **is** in the seventh grade.

3b An *action verb* is a verb that expresses physical or mental action.

EXAMPLES Cara **built** a model airplane.
Remember your books!

3c A *transitive verb* is an action verb that expresses an action directed toward a person or thing.

EXAMPLES The grocer **helped** the customers.
Only the hardiest plants **survived** the frost.

With transitive verbs, the action passes from the doer—the subject—to the receiver of the action. Words that receive the action of transitive verbs are called *objects*.

3d An *intransitive verb* expresses action (or tells something about the subject) without passing the action to a receiver.

EXAMPLES The audience **clapped**.
His eyeglasses **shattered** on the pavement.

A verb may be transitive in one sentence and intransitive in another.

EXAMPLES Leta **sang** a song. [transitive]
Leta **sang** softly. [intransitive]

EXERCISE 1   Identifying Action Verbs

Underline the action verb in each sentence.

EX.   Dolphins <u>remember</u> sounds.

1. In San Francisco, we visited an aircraft carrier.
2. Throw the ball to the pitcher.
3. Yoshi saw the notice on the bulletin board.
4. Who waters the plants every day?
5. First, melt the butter in the skillet.

EXERCISE 2   Identifying Transitive and Intransitive Verbs

Identify the italicized action verbs by writing *T* for transitive or *I* for intransitive on the line before each sentence.

EX.　_T_　1.　*Look* carefully through the early morning mist.

_____　1.　The Statue of Liberty *stands* in New York Harbor.

_____　2.　The people of France *gave* the statue to the United States.

_____　3.　The French people *raised* most of the money themselves.

_____　4.　Frédéric Auguste Bartholdi *designed* the statue.

_____　5.　The statue *rises* above star-shaped Fort Wood.

EXERCISE 3   Writing Sentences with Transitive and Intransitive Verbs

Choose five verbs from the list below. Use each verb to write two sentences. In one sentence, use the verb as a transitive verb and underline its object. In the other, use the verb as an intransitive verb. You may use different tenses of the verb. Identify each verb by writing *transitive* or *intransitive*.

EX.　　　draw　Monet drew <u>sketches</u> of the waterlilies.　(transitive)
　　　　　　　 Monet drew quickly.　(intransitive)

　　bake　　forget　　join　　play　　stop　　turn　　watch

1. _____

　 _____

2. _____

　 _____

3. _____

　 _____

4. _____

　 _____

5. _____

　 _____

LINKING VERBS

3e   A *linking verb* is a verb that links, or connects, the subject of a sentence with a noun, a pronoun, or an adjective in the predicate.

EXAMPLES   Jin Young Ko **is** a golfer. [The verb *is* connects *golfer* with the subject *Jin Young Ko*.]

Most of the runners **seemed** tired after the race. [The verb *seemed* links *tired* with the subject *runners*.]

Linking Verbs Formed from the Verb *Be*		
am	has been	may be
is	have been	might be
are	had been	can be
was	will be	should be
were	shall be	would have been

Other Linking Verbs					
appear	become	feel	grow	look	remain
seem	smell	sound	stay	taste	turn

Some words may be either action verbs or linking verbs, depending on how they are used.

ACTION   Farmers **grow** a variety of crops.

LINKING   Children **grow** taller each year. [The verb links *taller* with the subject *children*.]

ACTION   **Look** at the seeds through the microscope.

LINKING   **Look** surprised! [The verb links *surprised* with the understood subject *you*.]

EXERCISE 4   Identifying Linking Verbs

Underline the linking verb in each sentence.

EX.   Her name <u>sounded</u> unfamiliar to me.

1. Is Kimiko a new student in our school?
2. At first, she appeared shy and nervous.
3. Like many recent immigrants, she often felt homesick.
4. After a few weeks at school, she became more confident.
5. With the support of her teacher and her fellow students, she grew comfortable in her new surroundings.
6. The English language now seems easier for her.
7. After having studied it for several years, Kimiko is fluent in Chinese.
8. In Japan, she had been a member of a gymnastics team.
9. The sport of gymnastics looks very difficult to me.
10. Maybe someday I can be a gymnast like Kimiko.

EXERCISE 5   Identifying Linking Verbs

Underline the linking verb in each sentence. Draw two lines under the two words connected by each linking verb.

EX.   <u>Mars</u> <u>was</u> the Roman <u>god</u> of war.

1. The planet Mars appears red in the nighttime sky.
2. It is smaller than Earth.
3. Throughout the ages, Mars has been a source of mystery.
4. An icecap at the planet's south pole remains frozen during the entire Martian year.
5. During autumn and winter, the icecap grows larger.

HELPING VERBS

3f   A *verb phrase* contains a main verb and one or more helping verbs.

EXAMPLES   Theo **did remember** his overdue books.
I **might have seen** your jacket in the cafeteria.
The painting **may have been painted** by Winslow Homer.

3g   A *helping verb* helps the main verb to express action or a state of being.

EXAMPLES   Soon, the judges *will be* **announcing** the winner.
The meat *should have been* **cooked** more thoroughly.

Helping Verbs					
am	is	are	was	were	be
being	been	have	has	had	do
does	did	may	might	must	can
could	shall	should	will	would	

Sometimes a verb phrase is interrupted by another part of speech, such as a pronoun or an adverb.

EXAMPLES   **Am** *I* **singing** only in the second act?
He **does** *not* **have** a new phone.

EXERCISE 6   Identifying Verb Phrases and Helping Verbs

Underline each verb phrase in the following paragraph. Draw a second line under the helping verb.

EX.   <u>Have</u> you ever <u>played</u> tennis?

[1] Tennis can be traced back to an old French game. [2] Over the years, the rules of the game have remained largely the same. [3] However, the players' equipment has changed greatly. [4] During the twelfth and thirteenth centuries, players would hit the ball with the palms of their hands. [5] The sheepskin ball was filled with sawdust. [6] Later, pieces of wood were used with gloved hands. [7] By the middle of the fifteenth century, strung rackets had been invented. [8] Today, many professional players do not use wooden rackets. [9] Modern racket frames are made from a combination of materials, such as fiberglass, graphite, and metal. [10] Different materials for stringing the racket have also been tried.

EXERCISE 7   Identifying Verb Phrases and Helping Verbs

Underline the verb phrases in the sentences below. Draw a second line under the helping verbs.

EX.   Abraham Lincoln <u>was born</u> in Kentucky.

1. By his eighth birthday, Lincoln had moved twice.

2. As a young man, he had become a lawyer.

3. By 1848, he had been elected to the United States Congress.

4. He was elected to the office of President of the United States in 1860.

5. He is remembered for his honesty.

6. Frederick Douglass was born roughly a decade after Abraham Lincoln.

7. Born to enslaved people in Maryland, Douglass never did know his birth date.

8. In his youth, he was secretly taught to read and write.

9. By the age of about 20, he had escaped to freedom.

10. He would eventually publish his autobiography and an important abolitionist newspaper.

ADVERBS

3h   **An *adverb* is a word that modifies a verb, an adjective, another adverb, or an entire clause or sentence.**

An adverb answers the following questions:

Where?	How often?	To what extent?
When?	*or*	*or*
How?	How long?	How much?

EXAMPLES   Greta moved **quietly**. [*Quietly* is an adverb modifying the verb *moved*; it tells *how.*]

The meeting ended **rather suddenly**. [*Rather* is an adverb modifying the adverb *suddenly*; it tells *to what extent. Suddenly* is an adverb modifying the verb *ended*; it tells *how.*]

I **often** write **very** long letters to my friends. [*Often* is an adverb modifying the verb *write*; it tells *how often. Very* is an adverb modifying the adjective *long*; it tells *to what extent.*]

Later, we went **inside**. [*Later* is an adverb modifying the verb *went*; it tells *when. Inside* is an adverb also modifying the verb *went*; it tells *where.*]

Words Often Used as Adverbs	
Where?	away, here, inside, near, there, up
When?	ago, later, next, now, soon, then
How?	clearly, easily, quietly, slowly
How often? or *How long?*	always, briefly, continuously, endlessly, forever, never, usually
To what extent? or *How much?*	almost, extremely, least, more, not, quite, so, too, very

Many adverbs end in *-ly*. These adverbs are formed by adding *-ly* to adjectives. However, some words ending in *-ly* are used as adjectives.

Adverbs Ending in *-ly*
loud + -ly = loudly
slow + -ly = slowly

Adjectives Ending in *-ly*		
daily	friendly	lively
early	kindly	lonely

EXERCISE 8   Identifying Adverbs

Underline the adverbs in the following sentences. Draw an arrow to the word that each adverb modifies. [Note: A sentence may contain more than one adverb.]

EX.   A <u>rather</u> large boat sailed <u>past</u>.

1. The denim skirt was too long and too expensive.
2. Was the sun shining then?
3. Emilio will soon call his relatives in Costa Rica.
4. Suddenly, giant hailstones pounded the area, and extremely high winds uprooted many trees.
5. Yesterday, the seventh-grade class visited the Smithsonian Institution in Washington, DC.
6. The huge tiger growled fiercely and angrily.
7. Later, the traffic in the city seemed unusually heavy.
8. My cat seldom goes outside.
9. Kamaria always does her homework before supper.
10. Our old clock works amazingly well.

EXERCISE 9   Choosing Adverbs to Modify Adjectives

The adverb *very* is used far too often to modify adjectives. Write five sentences that each use an adverb other than *very* to modify one of the adjectives below. Use a different adverb with each adjective.

EX.   strong   This elephant is incredibly strong.

clever	happy	neat	sweet	tired
perceptive	narrow	nervous	taller	valuable

1. _____

2. _____

3. _____

4. _____

5. _____

REVIEW EXERCISE

A. Identifying Action Verbs and Linking Verbs

Underline the verb in each sentence. Then, on the line before the sentence, identify the verb by writing *A* for action verb or *L* for linking verb. If the verb is a linking verb, double underline the two words that it connects.

EX. __L__   Not all <u>dinosaurs</u> <u>looked</u> <u>fierce</u>.

_____ 1. Can you picture a dinosaur in your mind?

_____ 2. These creatures roamed the planet for millions of years.

_____ 3. Dinosaurs had skeletons like those of birds.

_____ 4. Some of these skeletons have been preserved as fossils.

_____ 5. Like the skin of reptiles, dinosaur skin might have felt scaly.

_____ 6. Some meat-eating dinosaurs were huge.

_____ 7. The largest dinosaurs might have been warm-blooded.

_____ 8. Some plant-eaters were the size of chickens.

_____ 9. Scientists do not know the color of dinosaurs.

_____ 10. The true appearance of dinosaurs will probably remain a mystery.

B. Writing Adverbs

Rewrite the following sentences. Make them more precise by adding to sentence an adverb that answers the question in parentheses.

EX.   The teacher gave the instructions. (how?)
         <u>The teacher gave the instructions slowly.</u>

1. The team had gone to the stadium. (when?)

    _____

2. It was an enjoyable trip. (to what extent?)

    _____

3. The deer ran across the meadow. (how?)

    _____

4. During the storm, the girls went. (where?)

    _____

5. Did Carlos buy the tickets? (when?)

    _____

3i A *preposition* is a word that shows the relationship between a noun or a pronoun and another word in the sentence.

Notice how changing the prepositions in the following sentences changes the relationship of *Martha* to *lake* and of *bushes* to *house*.

EXAMPLES   Martha walked **beside** the lake.
Martha walked **to** the lake.
Martha walked **toward** the lake.

The bushes **around** the house need trimming.
The bushes **behind** the house need trimming.
The bushes **in front of** the house need trimming.

Commonly Used Prepositions				
aboard	before	for	off	toward
about	behind	from	on	under
above	below	in	out	underneath
across	beneath	in front of	out of	unlike
after	beside	inside	over	until
against	between	instead of	past	up
along	beyond	into	since	up to
among	by	like	through	upon
around	down	near	throughout	with
as	during	next to	till	within
at	except	of	to	without

Some words may be used as prepositions or as adverbs. Remember that a preposition always has an object. An adverb never does. If you can't tell whether a word is used as an adverb or a preposition, look for an object.

PREPOSITION   I climbed **aboard** the ship. [*Ship* is the object of the preposition *aboard*.]

ADVERB   I climbed **aboard**. [*Aboard* is an adverb modifying the verb *climbed*; it tells *where*.]

EXERCISE 10   Writing Prepositions

Write a different preposition on the line in each sentence below.

EX.   My poodle lay __on__ the sofa.

1. The person _____ the counter is the owner.
2. Several sheep were grazing _____ the fence.
3. The helicopter flew _____ the clouds.
4. The woman who lives _____ us plays the oboe.
5. Your napkin is lying _____ the table.
6. The books _____ my desk are overdue at the library.
7. The flowers _____ the house bloomed early.
8. I looked _____ my brother when I came home.
9. Please meet me _____ the science museum.
10. The painting _____ the mantel was created by my great-aunt.

EXERCISE 11   Identifying Adverbs and Prepositions

Identify the italicized word in each sentence as either an adverb or a preposition. On the line, write *A* for adverb or *P* for preposition.

EX. __P__   Is the story of John Henry based *on* an actual event?

_____ 1. *In* American folklore, John Henry is a legendary character.
_____ 2. This African American hero became the Paul Bunyan *of* railroad construction.
_____ 3. Using a hammer, he pounded steel spikes *down* into rocks.
_____ 4. Other steel drivers were amazed *by* his strength.
_____ 5. Spectators came from miles *around* to watch him compete against a machine.

CONJUNCTIONS AND INTERJECTIONS

3j   A *conjunction* is a word that joins words or groups of words.

(1)   *Coordinating conjunctions* connect words or groups of words used in the same way.

Coordinating Conjunctions						
and	but	for	nor	or	so	yet

EXAMPLES   bridges **or** tunnels [two nouns]
powerful **yet** gentle [two adjectives]
before recess **and** after lunch [two prepositional phrases]
The alarm didn't go off, **so** I was late for school. [two complete ideas]

(2)   *Subordinating conjunctions* are used to introduce a subordinate clause.

Subordinating Conjunctions						
after	although	as if	as soon as	because	before	if
since	than	unless	until	when	wherever	while

EXAMPLES   **When** I visited Mexico last summer, I saw several beautiful murals.
Although the United States is more than 200 years old, many Europeans think of it as a young country.
Before they arrived at the camp, they had to climb the mountain.
As soon as the alarm goes off, I will get out of bed.

(3)   *Correlative conjunctions* are pairs of conjunctions that connect words or groups of words used in the same way.

Correlative Conjunctions						
both/and	either/or	neither/nor	no sooner/than	not/but	not only/but also	whether/or

EXAMPLES   **Both** Jupiter **and** Saturn have rings. [two nouns]
We will go **either** to the movies **or** to the ball game. [two prepositional phrases]
Not only did Wilma play the piano, **but** she **also** sang two songs. [two complete ideas]

EXERCISE 12   Identifying Conjunctions

Underline the conjunction in each sentence. [Note: A sentence may contain more than one conjunction.]

EX.   That animal is <u>either</u> an alligator <u>or</u> a crocodile.

1. Both the alligator and the crocodile are reptiles.

2. A crocodile has fewer but sharper teeth than the alligator.

3. Not only are crocodiles more vicious, but they are also more active than alligators.
4. These reptiles look alike, yet it is easy to tell them apart.
5. Neither alligators nor crocodiles are found in many areas, because they have been widely hunted.
6. While the guide was explaining the route to us, we saw a crocodile swim across the swamp.
7. Although it was only May, the temperature was over 90 degrees.
8. No sooner did we leave the car than we started sweating.
9. It was a fun yet exhausting day!
10. We learned a lot about alligators and crocodiles.

INTERJECTIONS

3k   An *interjection* **is a word that expresses strong emotion.**

An interjection has no grammatical relationship to the rest of the sentence. Usually, an interjection is followed by an exclamation point.

EXAMPLES   **Wow**! That sounds exciting.
                 Ouch! I just stubbed my toe.

Sometimes an interjection is set off by a comma or commas.
EXAMPLES   **Ugh,** these books are heavy.
                 That should take, **oh**, one hour to complete.

EXERCISE 13   Writing Interjections

You have just seen an exciting superhero movie. Write five sentences about the movie. In each sentence, use a different interjection from the list below. Underline the interjections that you use. [Remember that an interjection may be set off either by an exclamation point or by a comma or commas.]

EX.   <u>Aha!</u> I know who the villain is.
oh   oops   ouch   ugh   well   wow   yes

1. _____

2. _____

3. _____

4. _____

5. _____

MODULE REVIEW

A. Identifying Verbs, Adverbs, Prepositions, Conjunctions, and Interjections

Identify the part of speech of each italicized word. On the line before each sentence, write *V* for verbs, *A* for adverbs, *P* for prepositions, *C* for conjunctions, and *I* for interjections.

EX. __A__ Have you *ever* seen the strong man at a circus?

_____ 1. Circus strong men can *bend* steel with their bare hands.

_____ 2. *Well,* a blacksmith can bend steel also.

_____ 3. Many years ago, blacksmiths supplied people *with* a variety of everyday items.

_____ 4. They made cooking utensils, tools, plows, and *sometimes* even metal toys.

_____ 5. Today, factories make most of the metal products on the market, *but* not all of them.

_____ 6. *Surprise!* Blacksmiths are still at work in some places.

_____ 7. Their *most* important piece of equipment is a forge.

_____ 8. The blacksmith *heats* metal in the forge.

_____ 9. Then the softened metal is shaped by being hammered *or* pressed.

_____ 10. Plunging the hot metal *into* water cools the metal so that it keeps its new form.

B. Identifying Action Verbs and Linking Verbs

In the following sentences, underline each action verb and double underline each linking verb.

EX. Sonya <u>brought</u> her bike to a local shop for repairs.
The tire <u>had been</u> flat for a week.

1. Wenona carried her books to school.
2. Annie and Lily gave Roscoe their calculator.
3. Jesse helped me with the problem.
4. A pigeon is building its nest on the platform.
5. The twins are moving to Oregon in the fall.
6. Chicken soup tastes wonderful.
7. Marini has become a leader in her class.
8. Derrick showed his rock collection to the class on Thursday.
9. Vince, are you ready for the contest?
10. The bike is not new, but it is in excellent condition.

C.   Identifying Adverbs and Prepositions

In the sentences below, identify each italicized word as either an adverb or a preposition. On the line before each sentence, write *A* for adverb or *P* for preposition.

EX.   __A; P__   He watched *uneasily* as the deer walked *in* the garden.

_____ 1. Three people fell *off* the boat *suddenly*.

_____ 2. *Fortunately*, another boat was passing *by* when the accident happened.

_____ 3. The people who fell were *among* the many treated *for* injuries.

_____ 4. *At* the end of the trip, we were *repeatedly* asked to report what we had seen.

_____ 5. I had *never* been in a storm like that *before*.

D.   Writing Sentences

Write ten sentences that meet the following requirements. Underline the word that you are asked to use in each sentence, and identify how it is used.

EX.   Use *up* as an adverb and as a preposition.
         All the graduates stood up.—adverb
         The firefighter climbed up the ladder.—preposition

1. Use *daily* as an adjective and as an adverb.

   _____

   _____

2. Use *before* as an adverb and as a preposition.

   _____

   _____

3. Use *so* as an adverb and as a conjunction.

   _____

   _____

4. Use *yet* as a conjunction and as an adverb.

   _____

   _____

5. Use *well* as an interjection and as an adjective.

   _____

   _____

MODULE 4: COMPLEMENTS

DIRECT OBJECTS

4a   A *complement* is a word or a group of words that completes the meaning of a verb.

Every sentence has a subject and a verb. In addition, the verb often needs a complement to complete its meaning.

	s v
INCOMPLETE	Jared enjoys [*what?*]
	s v c
COMPLETE	Jared enjoys **tennis**.
	s v
INCOMPLETE	Jared is [*what?*]
	s v c
COMPLETE	Jared is **an athlete**.

A *direct object* is one type of complement. It completes the meaning of a transitive verb.

4b   A *direct object* is a noun or a pronoun that receives the action of a verb or shows the result of that action. A direct object answers the question *Whom?* or *What?* after a transitive verb.

EXAMPLES   The coach called **Lana**. [*Lana* receives the action of the verb *called* and tells *whom* the coach called.]

That company makes **equipment** for the sports team. [*Equipment* tells *what* the company makes.]

A direct object can never follow a linking verb because a linking verb does not express action. Also, a direct object is never part of a prepositional phrase.

LINKING VERB   Ms. Castillo **is** our tennis coach. [The verb *is* does not express action. Therefore, it has no direct object.]

PREPOSITIONAL PHRASE   She teaches **at our school**. [*School* is not the direct object of the verb *teaches*. It is the object in the prepositional phrase *at our school*.]

A direct object may be a compound of two or more objects.

EXAMPLE   I enjoy **tennis**, **baseball**, and **soccer**. [The compound direct object of the verb *enjoy* includes *tennis, baseball,* and *soccer*.]

EXERCISE 1   Identifying Direct Objects

Underline the direct object in each sentence. [Remember: A direct object may be compound.]

EX.   We watched a <u>video</u> about the migration of birds.

1. Jeremy walked the Henderson's dog each day for a week.
2. Henry lost his wallet and his jacket.
3. After rehearsal, Joni saw your brother at the swimming pool.
4. The school principal posted the rules on the bulletin board.
5. Last night, we streamed a movie.
6. As we listened, he answered our questions carefully.
7. I need directions to your house.
8. Ms. Martínez teaches Spanish and French at the high school.
9. Someone left a message on the table for you.
10. The cars and buses on the freeway pollute the air.

EXERCISE 2   Writing Sentences with Direct Objects

Complete each sentence by adding a direct object.

EX.   Georgio plays <u>basketball</u>.

1. Beatrice caught the _____.
2. I saw a _____ yesterday.
3. At the game, we met _____.
4. Jim kicked a _____.
5. The pitcher threw a _____.
6. Mimi won the _____.
7. At the end of the season, our team had a _____.
8. All of the players received _____.
9. At the banquet, the coach praised the _____.
10. Of all sports, I especially like _____.

MODULE 4: COMPLEMENTS

INDIRECT OBJECTS

An *indirect object* is another type of complement. Like a direct object, an indirect object helps to complete the meaning of a transitive verb. A sentence with an indirect object always has a direct object too.

4c　An *indirect object* **is a noun or pronoun that comes between a verb and a direct object. It tells** *to whom, to what, for whom,* **or** *for what* **the action of the verb is done.**

EXAMPLES　Dante gave **me** a gift. [The pronoun *me* is the indirect object of the verb *gave*. It answers the question *"To whom did Dante give a gift?"* The noun *gift* is the direct object.]

Ariana left **Tom** a note. [The noun *Tom* is the indirect object of the verb *left*. It answers the question *"For whom did Ariana leave a note?"* The noun *note* is the direct object.]

Like a direct object, an indirect object may be a compound of two or more objects.

EXAMPLE　He made his **mother** and **father** an anniversary card. [The nouns *mother* and *father* are the indirect objects of the verb *made*. They answer the question *"For whom did he make an anniversary card?"* The noun *card* is the direct object.]

NOTE　Linking verbs do not have indirect objects because they do not show action. Also, an indirect object is never part of a prepositional phrase.

INDIRECT OBJECT　Mr. Nguyen offered me a job.
PREPOSITIONAL PHRASE　Mr. Nguyen offered a job to me.

EXERCISE 3　Identifying Direct Objects and Indirect Objects

In each sentence, underline the direct object once. Underline the indirect object twice. [Remember: Objects may be compound.]

EX.　I loaned <u>Babette</u> my brown <u>boots</u>.

1. Hillary taught her dog a new trick.
2. I drew them a map of the town center.
3. Yesterday, my mother gave me a ride to school.
4. Helen read the class a poem by Langston Hughes.
5. Please tell us your new address.
6. During her vacation, my aunt sent me a postcard from Puerto Rico.
7. Harold told Kim and Filbert a story before their nap.
8. Sometimes Dr. Milano offers his neighbors vegetables from his garden.
9. Fortunately, the park ranger gave the hikers a warning about the mudslide.
10. I might give my little sister or my little brother this old jacket.

EXERCISE 4   Revising Sentences by Using Indirect Objects

Rewrite each sentence. Use the italicized information to write an indirect object. Underline the indirect objects in your revised sentences.

EX.   Mr. Desiderato gave an award *to Priya*.
Mr. Desiderato gave <u>Priya</u> an award.

1. Priya told the whole story *to us*.

   _____

2. Last month, she wrote a letter *to the city council*.

   _____

3. She gave *to them* several ideas about summer programs for kids.

   _____

4. They offered summer jobs *to Priya and her classmates*.

   _____

5. Together, the class taught many games *to the neighborhood children*.

   _____

6. They also offered swimming lessons *for the children*.

   _____

7. The city owed many thanks *to Priya* for her ideas and her organizational skills.

   _____

8. The neighborhood parents bought a trophy *for Priya*.

   _____

9. *For Priya and the swimming coaches,* all the children brought cards and banners.

   _____

10. Priya had given *to the city* a summer of fun.

   _____

PREDICATE NOMINATIVES

4d   A *subject complement* completes the meaning of a linking verb and identifies or describes the subject.

There are two kinds of subject complements—the *predicate nominative* and the *predicate adjective.*

EXAMPLES   Ricardo is the **leader** of the school jazz band. [*Leader* is the predicate nominative following the linking verb *is*. It identifies the subject *Ricardo*.]

The sun was **bright** this morning. [*Bright* is the predicate adjective following the linking verb *was*. It describes the subject *sun*.]

4e   A *predicate nominative* is a noun or pronoun that follows a linking verb and explains or identifies the subject of the sentence.

Like other subject complements, a predicate nominative may be compound.

EXAMPLES   A guanaco is a wild **animal** from South America. [*Animal* is a predicate nominative following the linking verb *is*. It explains the subject *guanaco*.]

Hiroshi became **treasurer** of our club. [*Treasurer* is the predicate nominative following the linking verb *became*. It identifies and explains the subject *Hiroshi*.]

The stars of the show might be **Greg** and **she**. [*Greg* and *she* are compound predicate nominatives following the linking verb *might be*. They identify the subject *stars*.]

NOTE   Be careful not to confuse a predicate nominative with a direct object. A predicate nominative always follows a linking verb, while a direct object always follows an action verb. Also, remember that a predicate nominative is never part of a prepositional phrase.

PREDICATE NOMINATIVE	Felicia is an artist.
DIRECT OBJECT	Felicia paints pictures.
PREPOSITIONAL PHRASE	Felicia may become famous as an artist.

EXERCISE 5   Identifying Predicate Nominatives and Linking Verbs

In each sentence, underline the linking verb once. Underline the predicate nominative twice.

EX.   Movies <u>are</u> great <u>entertainment</u>.

1. Some popular movies are remakes, not original ideas.
2. One example is the popular film *West Side Story*.
3. Two people, Robert Wise and Jerome Robbins, were the directors of the 1961 version.
4. Was their collaboration a success?
5. Rita Moreno is a talented actress, singer, and dancer.
6. Her best movies might be two adaptations of *West Side Story*.
7. Other stars in the 2021 version were Rachel Zegler and Ariana DeBose.
8. *West Side Story* is a modern version of the Shakespearean tragedy *Romeo and Juliet*.
9. Of the many songs in that movie, my favorites were "Tonight" and "Maria."
10. The composer of the music for *West Side Story* was Leonard Bernstein.

EXERCISE 6   Writing Sentences with Predicate Nominatives

Each of the following items is written as an equation. Rewrite each one as a sentence with a linking verb and a predicate nominative.

EX.   Maria Tallchief = ballerina
       <u>Maria Tallchief became a famous ballerina.</u>

1. dictionary = reference book

   _____

2. my best friends = Lisette and Jobelle

   _____

3. some industrial gases = argon, nitrogen, helium, neon

   _____

4. this rock = granite

   _____

5. winners of the award = Mina and I

   _____

MODULE 4: COMPLEMENTS
PREDICATE ADJECTIVES

4f A *predicate adjective* is an adjective that follows a linking verb and describes the subject of the sentence.

Like other complements, a predicate adjective may be compound.

EXAMPLES I felt **proud** about my report. [*Proud* is the predicate adjective that follows the linking verb *felt*. It describes the subject *I*.]

The apple was **red** and **shiny**. [*Red* and *shiny* are the predicate adjectives that follow the linking verb *was*. They describe the subject *apple*.]

EXERCISE 7 Identifying Predicate Adjectives and Linking Verbs

In each sentence below, underline the linking verb once. Underline the predicate adjective twice.

EX. That music <u>seems</u> too <u>loud</u>.

1. The vegetable soup smells good.
2. The sky is cloudy and dark today.
3. Your brother Reza is really funny!
4. During the drought, the lettuce in the garden became limp and wilted.
5. The hikers remained brave during the storm.

EXERCISE 8 Writing Sentences with Predicate Adjectives

Use five of the following nouns to write sentences. Use each noun as the subject of a sentence. Complete each sentence with a linking verb and a predicate adjective that describes the subject. Underline the predicate adjective in each of your sentences.

EX. traffic
The traffic was <u>heavy</u> on the freeway this morning.

| oranges | doctor | Julio | dinosaurs |
| dog | computers | soccer | English |

1. _____
2. _____
3. _____
4. _____
5. _____

REVIEW EXERCISE

A. Identifying Direct Objects, Predicate Nominatives, and Predicate Adjectives

On the line before each sentence, identify the word in italics by writing *DO* for *direct object, PN* for *predicate nominative,* or *PA* for *predicate adjective.*

EX. __DO__ The Aztecs spoke a *language* called Nahuatl.

_____ 1. They inhabited a *city* called Tenochtitlán, which is now the site of present-day Mexico City.

_____ 2. The jewelry and pottery that the Aztecs made were *important* to their trade with other peoples.

_____ 3. Recently, I became the *president* of the Spanish Club at school, and we held an Aztec Culture Fair.

_____ 4. I was almost *late* to the fair because I was making tamales.

_____ 5. Visitors to the fair enjoyed *representations* of Aztec culture, including food and artwork.

B. Writing Sentences with Complements

Write five sentences that might be clues for a crossword puzzle about volcanoes. In the first column, write sentences with blanks to show where the complements belong. In the second column, list the complements that you left out of your sentences. After each complement, write what kind of complement it is.

EX.   CROSSWORD CLUES   ANSWER KEY
        Volcanoes throw _____ into the air.   lava—direct object

1. _____   1. _____

2. _____   2. _____

3. _____   3. _____

4. _____   4. _____

5. _____   5. _____

MODULE REVIEW

A. Identifying and Classifying Complements

Underline each complement in the sentences below. On the line before each sentence, identify the complement by writing *DO* for *direct object, IO* for *indirect object, PN* for *predicate nominative,* or *PA* for *predicate adjective.* [Remember: Complements may be compound.]

EX. _IO; DO_   Jack gave <u>me</u> an <u>article</u> about Rachel Davis DuBois.

_____ 1. Rachel Davis DuBois was an important American teacher.

_____ 2. As a Quaker, Dr. DuBois had strong feelings about equality and human rights.

_____ 3. She developed a worldwide program for education and communication.

_____ 4. The basic idea behind her program seemed simple and wise.

_____ 5. She gathered people of different ethnic backgrounds for conversation and sharing.

_____ 6. Through her sessions, people became more knowledgeable about each other.

_____ 7. Knowledge and understanding gave them a better chance for living and working together peacefully.

_____ 8. The name of the program was "Group Conversation."

_____ 9. Some of the people she talked with were Martin Luther King Jr., Eleanor Roosevelt, and George Washington Carver.

_____ 10. The NAACP and the State Department have used Dr. DuBois's program both in the United States and throughout the world.

B. Writing Sentences with Complements

Each of the following items is an unfinished sentence. Write a complete version of the sentence adding words to create the type of complement shown in parentheses. Underline the complements in your completed sentences.

EX.   Ralph gave (indirect object) a (direct object).
        Ralph gave <u>Jamar</u> a <u>ticket</u> to the concert.

1. My favorite singer is (predicate nominative).

   _____

   _____

2. The river is (compound predicate adjective).

   _____

   _____

3. Ms. Robinson made (compound indirect object) some (direct object).

   _____

   _____

4. Two important historical figures are (compound predicate nominative).

   _____

   _____

5. The weather today is (predicate adjective).

   _____

   _____

MODULE 5: THE PHRASE

PREPOSITIONAL PHRASES

5a A *phrase* is a group of related words that is used as a single part of speech. A phrase may contain a subject or a verb, but not both.

EXAMPLES   will be studying [phrase, no subject]
           from that country [phrase, no subject or verb]

5b A *prepositional phrase* is a group of words consisting of a preposition, a noun or pronoun that serves as the object of the preposition, and any modifiers of that object.

A preposition is used to show the relationship between a noun or a pronoun and another word in a sentence.

EXAMPLES   The boat **on the water** was swaying. (The noun *water* is the object of the preposition *on.*)

           For this reason, I am trying to finish the race. (The noun *reason* is the object of the preposition *For.*)

           Will the hikers go **into the wilderness**? (The noun *wilderness* is the object of the preposition *into*.)

The object of a preposition may be compound.

EXAMPLES   Are you going to the concert **with Atul** and **Mady**?
           The judges divided the prize money **between them** and **us**.

EXERCISE 1   Identifying Prepositions and Prepositional Phrases

Underline the prepositional phrases in the following sentences. Double underline the preposition in each phrase.

    EX.   Children often like shoes <u>with colorful designs</u>.

1. Some people think about comfort when they buy shoes.
2. Others are more interested in a shoe's style and color.
3. Over the years, fashion has influenced shoe styles.
4. Ancient Romans wore high boots with open toes.
5. Only the emperor of Rome could wear purple boots.
6. Did you know that during the Middle Ages soft leather shoes were popular?
7. Lords and ladies walked in wide, floppy shoes.
8. Knights had long toe pieces on their armor.
9. Hip boots gave protection from rough weather.
10. In recent years, sneakers with fancy designs and bright colors have become popular.

EXERCISE 2   Identifying Prepositional Phrases and Objects of Prepositions

Underline the prepositional phrases in the sentences below. Double underline the object of the preposition in each phrase.

EX.   Jonas and I often go <u>to the park</u>.

1. No one except Rosa completed the assignment.
2. Prizes will be awarded to them tomorrow.
3. The first African American governor of a state was Louisiana's P.B.S. Pinchback.
4. The largest animal in the world is the blue whale.
5. We met many immigrants from Southeast Asia.

EXERCISE 3   Writing Sentences with Prepositional Phrases

Write a sentence using each of the following prepositional phrases. Underline the phrase in each sentence.

EX.   by the wind
        The red-and-blue fishing boat was tossed <u>by the wind</u>.

1. under his hat

   _____

2. at that moment

   _____

3. with brown eyes

   _____

4. of the city

   _____

5. to the mall

   _____

MODULE 5: THE PHRASE

ADJECTIVE PHRASES

5c   An *adjective phrase* modifies a noun or a pronoun.

A prepositional phrase used as an adjective is called an *adjective phrase*.

ADJECTIVE   The **concerned** children participated in a program to clean up the park.

ADJECTIVE PHRASE   The children **of Washington Middle School** participated in a program to clean up the park.

Adjective phrases answer the same questions that single-word adjectives answer.

What kind?	*Which one?*
How many?	*How much?*

EXAMPLES   I took a photograph **of my aunt**. [The prepositional phrase *of my aunt* is used as an adjective to modify the noun *photograph*. The phrase answers the question *What kind?*]

His rowboat is the one **with the red hull**. [*With the red hull* is used as an adjective to modify the pronoun *one*. The phrase answers the question *Which one?*]

That box **of CDs on the table** is Grandpa's. [The two adjective phrases *of CDs* and *on the table* modify the noun *box*. Both phrases answer the question *Which one?*]

The painting **of the girl with the black hair** was sold. [The adjective phrase *of the girl* modifies the noun *painting*, and answers the question *Which one?* The adjective phrase *with the black hair* modifies the noun *girl*, the object of the preposition in the first phrase, and answers the question *Which one?*]

EXERCISE 4   Identifying Adjective Phrases

Underline the adjective phrase in each sentence and draw an arrow from the phrase to the word it modifies. [Note: A sentence may contain more than one phrase.]

EX.   Cesar Chavez was the subject <u>of the news story</u>.

1. The man in the photograph was Cesar Chavez.

2. His contributions to society are well known.

3. A series of migrant labor camps was the scene of his youth.

4. He always wanted better working conditions for migrant farm workers.

5. He believed that dedication to them was important.

6. The grape pickers held a long strike against the California growers.

7. Chavez was one of the strike leaders.

8. Chavez was the organizer of the United Farm Workers.

9. Stories about Chavez's early struggles make interesting reading.

10. Have you read any articles about him?

EXERCISE 5   Identifying Adjective Phrases

Underline the adjective phrases in the paragraph below, and draw an arrow from each phrase to the word that it modifies. [Note: A sentence may contain more than one phrase.]

EX.   The waves on the ocean were foamy.

[1] I'll never forget the view of the seaside town. [2] Houses of whitewashed stone lined the winding road to the pier. [3] Children played and bought paper kites with long tails. [4] Later, a boat docked, bringing a crowd of noisy tourists with sunburned faces. [5] Their arrival meant our peaceful visit to the seashore had ended.

EXERCISE 6   Using Adjective Phrases

Write a sentence using each of the following prepositional phrases as an adjective phrase. Underline the phrase in each sentence.

EX.   of the supermarket
           The owner of the supermarket opened the store early.

1. with long legs

   _____

2. on the green carpet

   _____

3. of South America

   _____

4. about sports and medicine

   _____

5. between the four students

   _____

ADVERB PHRASES

5d   An *adverb phrase* modifies a verb, an adjective, or another adverb.

A prepositional phrase used as an adverb is called an *adverb phrase*.

ADVERB	The shoppers hurried **home**.
ADVERB PHRASE	The shoppers hurried **toward the exit**.

Adverb phrases answer the same questions that single-word adverbs answer.

When?	How?	To what extent?
Where?	How often?	How much?

EXAMPLES   Paris is famous **for its restaurants**. [The adverb phrase *for its restaurants* modifies the adjective *famous*, telling *how*.]

The meeting ran late **into the night**. [The adverb phrase *into the night* modifies the adverb *late,* telling *when* or *how*.]

We planted roses **beside the house**. [The adverb phrase *beside the house* modifies the verb *planted*, telling *where*.]

Notice that, unlike most adjective phrases, adverb phrases can appear at various places in sentences.

EXAMPLE   **Beside the house**, we planted roses.

EXERCISE 7   Identifying Adverb Phrases

Underline the adverb phrase in each sentence and draw an arrow to the word it modifies. [Note: A sentence may contain more than one phrase.]

EX.   Some birds fly south <u>for the winter</u>.

1. Animal migrations are common in nature.

2. Some animals can travel for long periods.

3. Across northern Canada, caribou migrate often.

4. These large deer live in herds.

5. Each spring, the animals move into open areas and look for food.

6. As winter approaches, the caribou head for the woods.

7. They feed on small plants called lichens.

8. The monarch butterfly looks fragile, but it can fly for great distances.

9. In a single year, some monarchs travel 4,000 miles.

10. However, the insects die soon after the long trip.

11. Arctic terns nest near the Arctic Circle.

12. The terns leave for Antarctica in the autumn.

13. With small radios, scientists have mapped the terns' routes.

14. During its lifetime, a tern may travel a million miles or more.

15. A tern's pointed wings carry it over long distances.

EXERCISE 8   Using Adverb Phrases

Select five phrases from the list below. Use each one as an adverb phrase in a sentence. Underline each adverb phrase, and double underline the word or words each phrase modifies.

    EX.   with great force
              The hurricane <u>hit</u> the city <u>with great force</u>.

in the rain forest	at four o'clock
with her savings	by the team
under the old bed	after the long movie

1. _____

2. _____

3. _____

4. _____

5. _____

REVIEW EXERCISE 1

A. Identifying Prepositional Phrases, Prepositions, and Objects

In the paragraph below, underline the prepositional phrases. In each phrase, draw a second line under the preposition, and circle the object of the preposition. [Note: A sentence may contain more than one prepositional phrase.]

EX.   Working with planes can be interesting.

[1] Monday was an important day in Mei-Ling's life. [2] She enlisted in the Air Force.

[3] Mei-Ling will soon be stationed near Los Angeles. [4] During the first weeks, she will go

through basic training. [5] After that time, she will take several tests to qualify for certain jobs.

[6] Mei-Ling will then transfer to a special school. [7] She would like a job in radar.

[8] However, she is also considering the field of space medicine. [9] Within a few months, she

will be given her choice of assignments. [10] Mei-Ling can then expect to have a long career in

the Air Force.

B. Identifying and Classifying Prepositional Phrases

In the sentences below, underline each prepositional phrase, and classify it as an *adjective phrase* or an *adverb phrase* by writing *ADJ* or *ADV* on the line before the sentence. Then double underline the word or words the phrase modifies.

EX.   _ADJ_   Do you know anything about space travel?

_____ 1. Life in a spacecraft requires much planning.
_____ 2. An air conditioner removes carbon dioxide from the air.
_____ 3. It also keeps the temperature of the air constant.
_____ 4. Weightlessness is a difficult problem for astronauts.
_____ 5. On long space missions, astronauts must exercise regularly.

5e   A *verb phrase* combines an action verb or a linking verb with one or more auxiliary, or helping, verbs.

EXAMPLES   He **has been swimming** for an hour. [The action verb is *swimming*, and the helping verbs are *has* and *been*.]

I **will buy** a cookbook for my brother. [The action verb is *buy*, and the helping verb is *will*.]

Bernice **should be** the team's captain. [The linking verb is *be*, and the helping verb is *should*.]

NOTE   The parts of a verb phrase may be separated by other words.

    EXAMPLES   **Have** you **changed** your mind?
                  He **did** not **know** the answer.

5f   A *verbal* is a verb form used as a noun, an adjective, or an adverb. Do not confuse verbals with verbs.

EXAMPLES   **Swimming** is good exercise. [*Swimming* is a verbal used as a noun.]

The **waxed** floors were slippery. [*Waxed* is a verbal used as an adjective to describe *floors*.]

To arrive at daybreak, the emergency supplies must be flown out before ten o'clock. [*To arrive* is a verbal used as an adverb to modify the verb phrase *must be flown*.]

EXERCISE 9   Identifying Verb Phrases and Verbals

Identify the italicized words in each sentence by writing *V* for verbal or *VP* for verb phrase on the line before the sentence.

EX.   <u> V </u>   a.   *Eating* watermelon is fun.
     <u> VP </u>   b.   The man *is eating* watermelon for breakfast.

<u>   </u>   1. a.   *Replacing* the food was expensive for the shopkeeper.
             b.   The shopkeepers *were replacing* the food in their stores.
<u>   </u>

_____ 2. a. Ethan wants *to shop* at the mall on Saturday.

_____   b. Ethan *will shop* at the mall on Saturday.

_____ 3. a. Jakayla *was giving* the closing speech.

_____   b. Jakayla likes *giving* the closing speech.

_____ 4. a. She *will take* your orders.

_____   b. By *taking* our orders, she helped the hostess.

_____ 5. a. *Losing* the dogs' leashes caused many problems for the trainers.

_____   b. The trainers *have lost* the dogs' leashes.

EXERCISE 10   Using Verb Phrases and Verbals

Use the verb given before each pair of sentences to create a verb phrase and a verbal that will complete the meaning of the sentences. Remember to add helping verbs to create verb phrases.

EX. rest   a. The <u>resting</u> dog stretched its back feet.

           b. The team <u>is resting</u> before the last match.

drive 1. a. Mr. Torres _____ his new car last night.

        b. The _____ rain caused floods in the valley.

hide 2. a. The boys looked for hours for the _____ toy.

        b. For this game, Miriam _____ under the bed.

lose 3. a. The _____ earring was found by Maria.

        b. We _____ money on this project.

cook 4. a. Aunt Salema _____ the dinner this year.

        b. We all enjoyed the juicy, _____ meat.

worry 5. a. _____ is simply a waste of time.

        b. The students _____ about their tests.

PARTICIPLES AND PARTICIPIAL PHRASES

THE PARTICIPLE

5g   A *participle* is a verb form that can be used as an adjective.

There are two kinds of participles: *present participles* and *past participles.*

(1)   *Present participles* end in *-ing.*

EXAMPLES   The detective searched for the **missing** necklace. [*Missing* is the present participle of the verb *miss.* The participle modifies the noun *necklace.*]

The **barking** dogs chased the truck. [*Barking* is the present participle of the verb *bark.* The participle acts as an adjective modifying the noun *dogs.*]

(2)   *Past participles* usually end in *-d* or *-ed.*

EXAMPLES   When he saw the **broken** bat, Spiro cried. [The irregular past participle *broken* modifies the noun *bat.*]

Disliked by the public, the television show was canceled. [The past participle *Disliked* modifies the noun *show.*]

EXERCISE 11   Identifying Participles and the Words They Modify

Underline the participles used as adjectives in the following sentences. Then double underline the noun or pronoun each participle modifies.

EX.   The <u>chirping</u> <u>birds</u> woke us up.

1. A fallen tree blocked our path.
2. The tourist took a photograph of the setting sun.
3. The men searched the ruins for the buried treasure of the pharaohs.
4. Deep in the jungle, the explorers found a deserted village.
5. Mr. Ling held the winning ticket in his hand.

PARTICIPIAL PHRASES

5h A *participial phrase* consists of a participle together with its modifiers and complements. The entire phrase is used as an adjective.

A participial phrase should be placed close to the word it modifies. Otherwise, the phrase may appear to modify another word, and the sentence may not make sense.

EXAMPLES **Humming softly**, she swept the sidewalk. [The participle *humming* is modified by the adverb *softly*. *Humming softly* is used as an adjective to modify the subject *she*.]

The directions, **written in Spanish**, were difficult for me to read. [The participle *written* is modified by the prepositional phrase *in Spanish*. *Written in Spanish* is used as an adjective to modify the subject *directions*.]

EXERCISE 12   Identifying Participial Phrases

Underline the participial phrase in each sentence. Then draw an arrow from the phrase to the word or words that it modifies.

EX.   Two cowboys, <u>riding on a snowy day</u>, stumbled upon Mesa Verde.

1. The ruins, lining the canyons, seemed to rise out of the rock.

2. Dating from the thirteenth century, they remain a wonderful sight.

3. The ruins, known as pueblos, were home to the Anasazi, ancestors of today's Pueblo peoples.

4. Developing their skills, the people became expert stoneworkers.

5. The people, working hard, built their homes in rocky terrain.

6. Chaco Canyon's Pueblo Bonita, started in 920 CE, had several hundred rooms.

7. Pueblo Bonita was five stories high with ladders connecting each level.

8. The Anasazi, using dry-land farming, raised beans and squash.

9. A drought lasting for many years may have forced them to move.

10. Abandoning these homes, the Anasazi moved to new villages south and east of their earlier dwellings.

MODULE 5: THE PHRASE

INFINITIVES AND INFINITIVE PHRASES

THE INFINITIVE

5i   An *infinitive* is a verb form, usually preceded by *to*, that can be used as a noun, an adjective, or an adverb.

EXAMPLES   I want **to try**. [*To try* is an infinitive used as a noun. It is the direct object of the verb *want*.]

Anna is the one **to ask**. [*To ask* is an infinitive used as an adjective. It modifies the pronoun *one*.]

Are you well enough **to run**? [*To run* is an infinitive used as an adverb. It modifies the adverb *enough*.]

NOTE   *To* plus a noun or a pronoun (*to Jaime, to me*) is a prepositional phrase, not an infinitive.

EXERCISE 13   Identifying Infinitives

Underline the infinitive in each sentence below.

EX.   Is this game easy <u>to play</u>?

1. Would you like to travel across the ocean on a boat?
2. Having large brains, dolphins are quick to learn.
3. To leave so early during the performance would be rude.
4. Those are the poems to memorize for speech class.
5. To prepare for the test, Hala studied for two hours.
6. How expensive is this bicycle tire to repair?
7. To escape the snarling lion was Nora's only thought.
8. Wong needs to practice his part for the play.
9. To succeed, you must study every day.
10. It was exciting to read the novel by Veronica Roth.

INFINITIVE PHRASES

5j An *infinitive phrase* consists of an infinitive together with its modifiers and complements. The entire phrase may be used as a noun, an adjective, or an adverb.

EXAMPLES **To design a computer program** takes skill. [The infinitive phrase is used as a noun. The infinitive *to design* has a complement, *a computer program*.]

Which is the best stroller **to buy for a baby**? [The infinitive phrase is used as an adjective to modify the noun *stroller*. The infinitive *to buy* is modified by the prepositional phrase *for a baby*.]

It was exciting **to win at chess yesterday**. [The infinitive phrase is used as an adverb to modify the adjective *exciting*. The infinitive *to win* is modified by the prepositional phrase *at chess* and by the adverb *yesterday*.]

EXERCISE 14 Identifying Infinitive Phrases

Underline the infinitive phrase in each sentence below.

EX. Lizards are interesting <u>to study in school</u>.

[1] Lizards are able to protect themselves in many ways. [2] Some lizards seem to match their surroundings. [3] The chameleon, for instance, likes to change its color for protection. [4] Other lizards like to play tricks on their enemies. [5] For example, some lizards will break off their tails to escape their enemies. [6] To replace their old tails, these lizards grow new ones. [7] A third way lizards defend themselves is to fly short distances. [8] The so-called flying dragon seems to sail from tree limb to tree limb. [9] Several lizards will fight to defend themselves. [10] One of these fighters, the monitor, thrashes its tail to whip its enemy.

REVIEW EXERCISE 2

A. Identifying and Classifying Participles and Infinitives

Underline the verbal in each sentence. Then identify it as participle or infinitive by writing *P* or *I* on the line before the sentence.

EX. __I__   Are you ready <u>to go</u>?

_____ 1. Exhausted, the hikers walked slowly into the camp.

_____ 2. Do you know the name of the person to interview?

_____ 3. The relay racers need time to rest.

_____ 4. Gloria put the frozen pizza into the oven.

_____ 5. The laughing children enjoyed the playfulness of the harp seals.

_____ 6. To succeed requires determination.

_____ 7. Most of the questions were easy to answer.

_____ 8. Broken glass was all over the cellar floor.

_____ 9. The librarian will help you to find a book about turtles.

_____ 10. Soccer can be a challenging sport.

B. Identifying and Classifying Participial and Infinitive Phrases

In each sentence, underline the participial phrase or the infinitive phrase. On the line before the sentence, label each phrase by writing *PP* for a participial phrase or *IP* for an infinitive phrase.

EX. __PP__   <u>Singing the song</u>, the children marched in the parade.

_____ 1. Jupiter takes almost twelve Earth years to circle the sun once.

_____ 2. It is hard to imagine a world like Jupiter.

_____ 3. Covered by thick clouds, its atmosphere is almost entirely liquid hydrogen.

_____ 4. The clouds, swirling constantly, form colorful belts or zones.

_____ 5. The Great Red Spot, discovered three centuries ago, lies near its equator.

_____ 6. According to astronomers, the red spot seems to vary in color.

_____ 7. From Earth, it is impossible to photograph the surface of Jupiter.

_____ 8. The Pioneer and Voyager series spacecrafts were launched to get a close-up view of the planet.

_____ 9. Moving at great speeds, the spaceships traveled for more than a year.

_____ 10. To reach the distant planet was an incredible accomplishment.

C. Writing a Paragraph Using Participial Phrases and Infinitive Phrases

As part of a social studies project, your class is compiling a photo essay about your community. You want to include a photograph and a description of your favorite place in the community. Your description should include answers to the questions below about your chosen place. Include either infinitive phrases or participial phrases in some of your sentences. Then underline and label each phrase.

QUESTIONS	SAMPLE RESPONSES
Where is this place?	beside the river; across the city bridge
Why is it special to you?	IP It's where I used to fish with my friends.
What sounds do you hear?	PP PP loudly chirping birds; cars honking at people
What do you see?	PP tall oak trees bending over; clear blue water

_____

_____

_____

_____

_____

_____

_____

_____

_____

_____

_____

_____

_____

MODULE REVIEW

A. Identifying Prepositions, Objects, and the Words Modified

In each sentence, find all of the prepositional phrases. Underline the preposition once and the object of the preposition twice. Then, on the line before each sentence, write the word or words the phrase modifies. [Note: A sentence may contain more than one phrase.]

EX. liked   On the farm, Mr. Orizini liked milking the cows.

_____ 1. Pioneer women made colorful quilts from fabric scraps.

_____ 2. A huge bowl of fruits decorated the table.

_____ 3. We often climb the hill behind our house.

_____ 4. During World War I, armies dug long trenches.

_____ 5. Some cacti can live for years without any water.

_____ 6. Early in the morning, we see Pedro jogging.

_____ 7. The difference between a toad and a frog is obvious.

_____ 8. A triangle is a polygon with three sides.

_____ 9. Instead of paste, please buy paper.

_____ 10. Holland is famous for its tulips.

B. Identifying Phrases

In the sentences below, underline all verbal phrases once, and double underline all prepositional phrases. [Note: A sentence may contain more than one phrase.]

EX.   Tourists love to visit Switzerland in the winter.

1. The Swiss mountains are popular spots for hot-air balloon trips.
2. Balloonists travel together on an adventurous trip.
3. Guided by wind currents, the balloon glides over the mountains.
4. To float over the snow-clad Alps is a marvelous experience.
5. I would never pass up the opportunity to make a hot-air balloon flight.

C.   Identifying Phrases

Underline the prepositional, participial, and infinitive phrases in the paragraph below. Label these phrases *PREP* for prepositional, *PART* for participial, or *INF* for infinitive. [Note: In this paragraph, *writing* is used as a noun, not a participle.]

                                    PREP   INF

EX.   Early civilizations used various types <u>of symbols</u> <u>to represent words</u>.

[1] To record language was a major step in civilization's development. [2] The Sumerians used the earliest system of true writing about 5,000 years ago. [3] Living in Mesopotamia, the Sumerians carefully pressed tools into wet clay tablets to make impressions. [4] This type of writing, known as cuneiform, was later refined by the Babylonians. [5] Today, scholars study cuneiform to learn the history of the Sumerians.

MODULE 6: THE CLAUSE
INDEPENDENT AND SUBORDINATE CLAUSES

6a **A *clause* is a group of words that contains a verb and its subject.**

Every clause contains a subject and a verb. However, not all clauses express complete thoughts.

6b **An *independent* (or *main*) *clause* expresses a complete thought and can stand by itself as a sentence.**

EXAMPLES   Gloria tied her sneakers.
She wore a red jersey.

When an independent clause stands alone, it is called a sentence. Usually, the term *independent clause* is used only when such a clause is joined with another clause.

SENTENCE   She leaped over the hurdle.

INDEPENDENT CLAUSE   When she reached the turn, **she leaped over the hurdle**.

6c **A *subordinate* (or *dependent*) *clause* does not express a complete thought and cannot stand alone.**

A subordinate clause must be joined with at least one independent clause to express a complete thought. Notice that words such as *since*, *that*, and *if* signal the beginning of a subordinate clause.

SUBORDINATE CLAUSES   since we moved here
that you will like
if the night is clear

SENTENCES   **Since we moved here**, I have learned to ski.
Rafael heard about a movie **that you will like**.
If the night is clear, you will see shooting stars.

EXERCISE 1   Identifying Independent and Subordinate Clauses

For each sentence, identify the italicized clause by writing *I* for independent or *S* for subordinate on the line before the sentence.

EX. _S_   Please bring your camera *when you visit*.

_____ 1. The tomatoes, *which we grew ourselves*, taste wonderful.
_____ 2. *Jennifer bought that dog* when it was just a puppy.
_____ 3. This is Diego, *whose sister you met yesterday*.

_____ 4. *If you need more paper*, I can give you some.

_____ 5. *Rain has fallen every weekend* since I bought my skates.

_____ 6. When the plane lands, *please stay in your seats*.

_____ 7. The door opened *as we walked up the stairs*.

_____ 8. *You can talk to Mr. Shankar* before class starts.

_____ 9. *The instrument* that you heard *is an oboe*.

_____ 10. Because you read quickly, *you can finish this story in an evening*.

EXERCISE 2   Writing Sentences with Subordinate Clauses

Add independent clauses to the following subordinate clauses to create sentences. Write your sentences on the lines after each clause. Underline the independent clause in each sentence.

EX.   because it is gold _____

        The statue will never rust because it is gold.
        _____

1. who wrote this report _____

    _____

2. when you're ready _____

    _____

3. as the winners were announced _____

    _____

4. if you want tickets to the concert _____

    _____

THE ADJECTIVE CLAUSE

6d   An *adjective clause* is a subordinate clause that modifies a noun or a pronoun.

Like an adjective or an adjective phrase, an adjective clause may modify a noun or a pronoun. Unlike an adjective phrase, an adjective clause contains a verb and its subject.

ADJECTIVE   a **big** computer

ADJECTIVE PHRASE   a computer **with a big screen** [does not have a verb and its subject]

ADJECTIVE CLAUSE   a computer **that has a big screen** [has a verb and its subject]

An adjective clause usually follows the noun or pronoun it modifies and tells *which one* or *what kind*.

EXAMPLES   The girl **who won the race** is my cousin. [The adjective clause modifies the noun *girl,* telling *which one*.]

I want a jacket **that zips up the front**. [The adjective clause modifies the noun *jacket*, telling *what kind*.]

An adjective clause is almost always introduced by a *relative pronoun*.

Relative Pronouns				
that	which	who	whom	whose

EXERCISE 3   Identifying Adjective Clauses

Underline the adjective clause in each sentence.

EX.   I played baseball, <u>which is my favorite sport</u>.

1. Maria Tallchief is the ballerina who founded the ballet company.
2. The conductor, who looked familiar, was a friend of my aunt.
3. This is the store that is having the sale on used books.
4. The photograph, which was taken in 1973, looks faded now.
5. The person whose name you have picked will be your partner.
6. At last, the surgeon, who looked tired, finished the operation.
7. The wok that I'm using belongs to Tanya.
8. I got a stain on this sweater, which belongs to my older sister.
9. Jason Reynolds is the author whom we met.
10. The keyboard that looks different is a new design.

EXERCISE 4   Identifying Adjective Clauses and Relative Pronouns

Underline the adjective clause in each sentence. Double underline the relative pronoun that begins the clause.

EX.   The woman <u>whose biography you read</u> was a great singer.

1. This is the first opera that I've seen.
2. The baritone is the man whose voice you hear.
3. The story, which is complicated, is explained in the program.
4. This is the character whom you saw in the first act.
5. All the songs that you heard were written by Scott Joplin.
6. The understudy who replaced the lead was Martina Arroyo.
7. Mr. Topin gave me a book that tells the plot of this opera.
8. One section of the stage, which moves up and down, creates that special effect.
9. The man who designed the sets is Mr. Virgli.
10. The music that you recognized is the theme song of a movie.

EXERCISE 5   Combining Sentences by Using Adjective Clauses

Rewrite each set of sentences below by making the second sentence into an adjective clause and adding it to the first sentence. Use the relative pronoun given in parentheses to begin the clause.

EX.   I have the book. The book belongs to Mei-Ling. (*that*)
       I have the book that belongs to Mei-Ling.

1. The runner is being interviewed. The runner won the race. (*who*)

   _____

2. Aunt Sylvia is a talented woman. I admire her. (*whom*)

   _____

3. Here is the soup. The soup is my favorite part of the meal. (*which*)

   _____

4. We studied an animal. The animal is extinct. (*that*)

   _____

5. A have a friend. My friend's dog is named Pokey. (*whose*)

   _____

THE ADVERB CLAUSE

6e   An *adverb clause* is a subordinate clause that modifies a verb, an adjective, or another adverb.

Like an adverb or an adverb phrase, an adverb clause may modify a verb, an adjective, or an adverb. Unlike an adverb phrase, an adverb clause contains a verb and its subject.

ADVERB   **Once**, Carl appeared in a movie.

ADVERB PHRASE **As a young boy**, Carl appeared in a movie. [does not have a verb and its subject]

ADVERB CLAUSE **When Carl was younger**, he appeared in a movie. [has a verb and its subject]

An adverb clause answers one of the following questions: *How? When? Where? Why? To what extent? How much? How long?* or *Under what conditions?*

EXAMPLES This statue looks **as if it were alive**. [The adverb clause tells *how* the statue looks.]

    Before you leave, look at this mobile. [The adverb clause tells *when* to look.]

    The artist collected shells **wherever she traveled**. [The adverb clause tells *where* she collected shells.]

    Because maple is a light wood, it goes well with ebony. [The adverb clause tells *why* maple goes well with ebony.]

    We can see the whole exhibit **if we stay until five**. [The adverb clause tells *under what conditions* we can see the whole exhibit.]

In these examples, notice that adverb clauses may be placed in various positions in sentences. When an adverb clause comes at the beginning of a sentence, it is usually followed by a comma.

Adverb clauses begin with *subordinating conjunctions*.

Common Subordinating Conjunctions			
after	as soon as	in order that	until
although	as though	since	when
as	because	so that	whenever
as if	before	than	where
as long as	how	though	wherever

NOTE Some subordinating conjunctions, such as *after, as, before, since,* and *until,* may also be used as prepositions.

EXERCISE 6   Identifying Adverb Clauses

Underline the adverb clause in each sentence below.

EX.   <u>When I read about astronomy</u>, I get excited.

1. Since I was in the first grade, I have been interested in space.
2. I read as much as I can about the planets.
3. I learned an interesting fact while I was reading about Pluto, a dwarf planet.
4. Before astronomers discovered Pluto's moon in 1978, they had not known the planet's size.
5. Although Pluto is tiny, it has three moons.
6. Because Pluto is small, it has little gravitational pull on its neighbors, Uranus and Neptune.
7. However, Neptune and Uranus wobble in orbit, as if some other small planet were nearby.
8. Scientists learned more about Pluto's surface when they used the Hubble Space Telescope to observe it.
9. When the New Horizons spacecraft flew near Pluto, astronomers learned more interesting facts about the dwarf planet.
10. Views of Pluto have been vastly improved since the James Webb Space Telescope was launched.

MODULE 6: THE CLAUSE
MODULE REVIEW

A. Identifying and Classifying Independent and Subordinate Clauses

Decide whether each of the following clauses is independent or subordinate. On the line before each clause, write *I* if the clause is independent or *S* if it is subordinate.

EX. __I__ the mahouts in India know a special language

__S__ because they work with elephants

_____ 1. wherever elephants are used to perform work

_____ 2. a mahout rides on the elephant's head

_____ 3. while the mahout gives the animal commands

_____ 4. since an elephant may understand dozens of commands

_____ 5. an elephant can lift heavy lumber

_____ 6. because the mahout's orders are given in a special language

_____ 7. whenever a mahout works with an elephant

_____ 8. these words are used only with elephants

_____ 9. although it may be an ancient Indian language

_____ 10. unless someone records this special language soon

B. Identifying and Classifying Subordinate Clauses

Underline the subordinate clause in each sentence. On the line before the sentence, write *ADJ* if the clause is an adjective clause or *ADV* if the clause is an adverb clause.

EX. __ADV__ <u>When you want to communicate with distant relatives</u>, you can use a telephone.

_____ 1. People used other methods of communication before they had telephones.

_____ 2. At one time, people probably used hollow logs that they hit with sticks.

_____ 3. The sound traveled to people who lived far away.

_____ 4. Later, they hit drums that were made from animal skins.

_____ 5. Because the drums were different shapes and sizes, they made different sounds.

_____ 6. Although sound was used by some people, other people used smoke signals.

_____ 7. This was one method that some Chinese, Egyptians, and Native Americans used.

_____ 8. However, smoke signals were hard to see if they were sent at night.

_____ 9. After electricity was discovered, many new forms of communication appeared.

_____ 10. Today, people who have smartphones can communicate with others around the world.

C. Writing Notes for an Oral Report

You are preparing to give an oral report called "The Building of the Pyramids at Giza." You need to prepare good notes to use during your report.

1. Gather information from a reliable online source or reference book.

2. Write notes on the following topics: where the pyramids are located; what they look like; how, why, and when they were built. In your notes, use five adjective clauses and five adverb clauses.

3. Underline and label the adjective and adverb clauses that you use.

EX. Giza—pyramid <u>that is best known</u> (adjective)

     construction began <u>before Pharaoh Khufu died</u> (adverb)

     Built to honor Khufu, <u>who was called Cheops by Greeks</u> (adjective)

_____

_____

_____

_____

_____

_____

_____

_____

_____

_____

_____

_____

_____

_____

_____

_____

_____

_____

_____

MODULE 7: SENTENCE STRUCTURE
SIMPLE SENTENCES

7a   A *simple sentence* has one independent clause and no subordinate clauses.

EXAMPLES   **Teresa ordered** a portable speaker online.

      Behind the house **grew** a small oak **tree**.

A simple sentence may have a compound subject, a compound verb, or both.

EXAMPLES   Both **vitamins** and **minerals are** important to your health. [compound subject]

      Jorge studied all of the facts and then **made** his decision. [compound verb]

      The **plumber** and her **helper replaced** the faucet and **fixed** the leak. [compound subject and compound verb]

EXERCISE 1   Identifying Subjects and Verbs in Simple Sentences

Underline the subject once and the verb twice in the following sentences. [Note: Some sentences may have a compound subject, a compound verb, or both.]

EX.   <u>South America</u> <u>is</u> about twice the size of the United States but <u>has</u> about the same number of people.

1. High mountains and tropical forests provide variety in the continent's climate.

2. The Andes Mountains separate Chile and Argentina.

3. The highest point in South America is Aconcagua.

4. Brazil's coastline stretches more than four thousand miles.

5. In South America, most people speak Spanish or Portuguese.

6. Manufacturing and mining in South America have grown rapidly and have become vital to the economy.

7. Plantations, farms, and ranches cover vast areas of the continent and employ about a third of all South Americans.

8. Coffee and bananas are two of the major crops of South America.

9. South America exports minerals and agricultural products and imports many manufactured goods.

10. Silver and copper are among South America's mineral exports.

11. Many different animals and birds live in the Amazon basin.

12. The capybara grows to four feet and is the world's largest rodent.

13. South America's largest snake, the anaconda, lives near water and swims in the rivers.

14. On the Galapagos Islands live giant turtles.

15. The hoglike tapir, about the size of a pony, is South America's largest wild animal.

EXERCISE 2   Writing Simple Sentences

On the lines below, write five simple sentences. In your sentences, use a compound subject, a compound verb, and both a compound subject and a compound verb. Underline all subjects once and all verbs twice.

EX.   My friends and I ate lunch and then went to a movie.

1. _____

_____

2. _____

_____

3. _____

_____

4. _____

_____

5. _____

_____

COMPOUND SENTENCES

7b   A *compound sentence* has two or more independent clauses and no subordinate clauses.

EXAMPLE   Chi Chen plays the trombone, and Mavis plays the saxophone. [*Chi Chen plays the trombone* and *Mavis plays the saxophone* are independent clauses.]

The independent clauses of a compound sentence are usually joined by a comma and a coordinating conjunction (*and, but, or, nor, for, so*, or *yet*).

NOTE   Do not use a comma if *for* is used as a preposition. Only use a comma before *for* when it is used as a conjunction combining two independent clauses (usually in formal situations).

The independent clauses of a compound sentence may be joined by a semicolon.

EXAMPLE   Rachel Carson was the author of *Silent Spring*; she also worked for the U.S. Fish and Wildlife Service.

The independent clauses may also be joined by a semicolon and a conjunctive adverb or a transitional expression, which is followed by a comma.

EXAMPLE   Gary Soto thought his first poems were awkward**; therefore**, he worked hard to improve his writing.

NOTE   A *compound sentence* is different from a simple sentence with a compound subject, or a compound verb, or both.

SIMPLE SENTENCE   **Nicholas went** to Rome in April and **stayed** at a small hotel near the Forum. [single subject and compound verb]

COMPOUND SENTENCE   **Nicholas went** to Rome in April, and **he stayed** at a small hotel near the Forum. [Both independent clauses have a single subject and a single verb.]

SIMPLE SENTENCE   **Hisoka** and **Tamara bought** some sandpaper and **refinished** the top of the table. [compound subject and compound verb]

COMPOUND SENTENCE   **Hisoka** and **Tamara bought** some sandpaper; later **they refinished** the top of the table. [The first independent clause has a compound subject and a single verb. The second independent clause has a single subject and a single verb.]

EXERCISE 3   Identifying Parts of Compound Sentences

Underline the subject once and the verb twice in each of the following independent clauses. Then circle each coordinating conjunction, semicolon, or conjunctive adverb.

EX.   <u>Scientists</u> <u><u>discovered</u></u> prehistoric cave paintings, (and) <u>they</u> also <u><u>found</u></u> stone tools and animal bones in caves.

1. Prehistoric people had not invented writing, so they could not record history.

2. Early people in cold climates made clothing from animal skins, yet the people could not stay warm enough without fires.

3. Ice sheets lowered sea levels; as a result, people traveled between regions on land bridges.

4. A gradual warming trend melted the ice sheets, so the seas began to cover the land bridges.

5. People would live for several weeks near a large source of food, so hunters often built shelters at campsites.

6. A campsite would be divided into sections; the group used some areas for preparing food, and other areas were used for sleeping.

7. Some campsites had garbage heaps, and these give scientists clues about tools, clothing, and food.

8. Many tools were made from stone; others were made of bone and wood.

9. Farming was not developed until around 10,000 BCE, so early people hunted animals and collected wild plants for food.

10. The first farmers grew crops, yet they still hunted for food.

11. Prehistoric hunters probably lived in groups of twenty-five to fifty persons, and each group consisted of several families.

12. The families shared the work of the group, but not all of the group's members hunted for food.

13. A hunting group moved from place to place, yet it rarely met another group.

14. Hunters developed new weapons and methods; therefore, larger animals could be captured and killed.

15. Scientists have pieced together a story of early human development, but many questions are still unanswered.

EXERCISE 4   Writing Compound Sentences

Write four compound sentences. Use a semicolon to join the independent clauses of your first sentence. Use the conjunctive adverb *therefore* in your second sentence. In your last two sentences, use the coordinating conjunctions *but* and *or*. Underline all subjects once and all verbs twice.

EX.   I take the bus to school, but my older sister drives.

1. _____

2. _____

3. _____

4. _____

EXERCISE 5   Distinguishing Compound Sentences from Compound Subjects or Compound Verbs

Identify each of the following sentences as either simple or compound. Write *S* for *simple* or *C* for *compound* on the line before the sentence. Then underline each subject once and each verb twice.

EX. _C_   The mosque is a place of worship; the Muslim community goes there to recite prayers.

_S_   A mosque may be a small tower or may include several buildings.

_____   1.   Muslims pray at the mosque on Fridays, and these special Friday mosques are often large buildings.

_____   2.   A courtyard and a prayer hall usually are important features of a Friday mosque.

_____   3.   The prayer hall has no seats; it has carpets instead.

_____   4.   The call to prayer at first was delivered from the roof of a house but now comes from a minaret, or tower.

_____   5.   Some Islamic countries have square minarets; others have spiral shapes.

EXERCISE 6   Writing Simple Sentences and Compound Sentences

Following the instructions for each item below, write simple and compound sentences. Underline each subject once and each verb twice.

EX.   compound sentence with a compound subject in the second independent clause

Basketball <u>tryouts</u> <u>are</u> tomorrow, but <u>Mara</u> and <u>Devon</u> <u>will be</u> out of town.

1. simple sentence with a compound subject _____

_____

2. simple sentence with a compound verb _____

_____

3. simple sentence with a compound subject and a compound verb

_____

_____

4. compound sentence with a compound subject in the first independent clause _____

_____

5. compound sentence with a compound verb in the second independent clause _____

_____

COMPLEX SENTENCES

7c   A *complex sentence* has one independent clause and at least one subordinate clause.

Two kinds of subordinate clauses are adjective clauses and adverb clauses. *Adjective clauses* usually begin with relative pronouns, such as *who, whose, which*, and *that. Adverb clauses* begin with subordinating conjunctions, such as *after, although, as, because, if, since, so that*, and *when*.

EXAMPLES   The student **who designed the stage set** is in my theater class. [complex sentence with an adjective clause]

Although they could not have known whether they would find land, Polynesians explored the vast Pacific Ocean in outrigger sailboats, using the stars and ocean swells to navigate. [complex sentence with an adverb clause]

If you want to make a tortilla, you need a very fine grade of cornmeal, **which is called** *masa harina* **in Mexico**. [complex sentence with an adverb clause and an adjective clause]

EXERCISE 7   Identifying Subordinate Clauses

Underline the subordinate clause in each of the following sentences. Then double underline the subordinating conjunction or the relative pronoun that begins the subordinate clause.

EX.   The white oak is a valuable tree <u>because its wood is used for floors and furniture</u>.

1. Native Americans who ate the acorns of the tree taught the European settlers about its importance as a food source.
2. The white oak, which can grow to a height of one hundred feet, is the state tree of Connecticut.
3. The people of the state chose the tree because it played an important role in the early history of the Connecticut colony.
4. In 1662, Charles II, who was king of England, granted a charter to the colony.
5. The charter that Charles II gave the colony served as the state's constitution until 1818.
6. Sir Edmund Andros, who was the governor of the Dominion of New England, tried to seize control of Connecticut.
7. When he arrived in Connecticut in 1687, he demanded the charter.
8. Since the colonists valued their freedom, they refused his demands.
9. Settlers hid the charter in the trunk of a white oak, which is now called the Charter Oak.
10. Although historians are not sure of all the facts, the story of the Charter Oak is always included in the history of Connecticut.

EXERCISE 8   Writing Complex Sentences

On the lines below, write five complex sentences. In your sentences, use subordinate clauses that begin with *because*, *when*, *though*, *who*, and *which*. Underline the subordinate clause in each sentence.

EX.   <u>When Roscoe finished his report</u>, he returned his reference books to the school library.

1. _____

2. _____

3. _____

4. _____

5. _____

MODULE 7: SENTENCE STRUCTURE
MODULE REVIEW

A. Identifying and Classifying Independent and Subordinate Clauses

In the following sentences, underline each independent clause once and each subordinate clause twice.

> EX. <u>Tet</u>, <u><u>which is the Vietnamese New Year</u></u>, <u>is a time of family gatherings and great celebration</u>.

1. Jim Thorpe, who was an amazing athlete, was descended mainly from the Sauk and Fox peoples.
2. Before Isabel gave her story to the editor, she proofread it.
3. As we watched the last few minutes of the game, the quarterback threw the ball down the field for a touchdown.
4. Robert Moses was commissioner of New York parks when the Verrazano-Narrows Bridge was built.
5. Because heavy winds whipped up the water in the bay, we headed for the harbor.
6. My brother pointed the remote control at the television set while he switched from channel to channel.
7. Although the grand piano was invented more than one hundred years ago, its overall shape has not changed.
8. Oases, which are fertile areas in the desert, vary in size.
9. Charlene wants a job this summer so that she can start saving money for college.
10. Jupiter, which is the fifth planet from the sun, is the largest planet in the solar system.

B. Identifying Simple, Compound, and Complex Sentences

Identify each of the following sentences as simple, compound, or complex. On the line before the sentence, write *S* for simple, *C* for compound, or *CX* for complex.

> EX. <u>CX</u> 1. While people have used many kinds of clocks, all clocks have been used to tell time.

_____ 1. Before clocks were invented, people studied the motions of the stars at night and checked the shadows on their sundials during the day.

_____ 2. Early Egyptians used water clocks, but in another early timepiece, the hourglass, sand was used.

_____ 3. The water clock was a clay bowl or glass jar with a scale of markings on its side.

_____ 4. As the water ran out, the water that was left in the jar marked the time.

_____ 5. The hourglass had two glass bulbs that were joined at a small opening.

_____ 6. The grains of sand flowed from the top bulb to the bottom bulb in about one hour.

     7. The first mechanical clocks in Western civilization, which were invented during the late 1200s, had no hands.

     8. Because the clock had no hands, it told the time with chiming bells.

     9. In the mid-1300s, Western inventors added an hour hand and a dial to the mechanical clock.

     10. By the 1920s, many homes had electric clocks; digital clocks gained popularity in the 1970s.

C. Writing Simple, Compound, and Complex Sentences

Write five sentences following the directions for each item below.

EX.   a simple sentence with a compound verb
       Rosa sawed the boards and nailed them in place.

1. a simple sentence

_____

_____

2. a simple sentence with a compound subject and a compound verb

_____

_____

3. a compound sentence with two independent clauses joined by the coordinating conjunction *and*

_____

_____

4. a compound sentence with two independent clauses joined by the coordinating conjunction *but*

_____

_____

5. a complex sentence

_____

_____

MODULE 8: AGREEMENT

AGREEMENT OF SUBJECT AND VERB

Number is the term used to describe the form of a word that indicates whether the word is singular or plural.

8a   When a word refers to one person, place, thing, or idea, it is *singular* in number. When a word refers to more than one, it is *plural* in number.

8b   A verb agrees with its subject in number.

Two words *agree* when they have the same number. The number of a verb must always agree with the number of its subject.

(1) Singular subjects take singular verbs.

EXAMPLE   The **flag flies** on holidays. [The singular verb *flies* agrees with the singular subject *flag*.]

(2) Plural subjects take plural verbs.

EXAMPLE   Some **trees change** color in the fall. [The plural verb *change* agrees with the plural subject *trees*.]

When a sentence contains a verb phrase, the first helping verb in the verb phrase agrees with the subject.

EXAMPLES   The **turtle is** racing.   The **flight has** been postponed.
            The **turtles are** racing.   The **flights have** been postponed.

EXERCISE 1   Recognizing Words as Singular or Plural

On the line before each of the following sentences, classify each italicized word by writing *S* for *singular* or *P* for *plural*.

EX. __C__   Our library *offers* a huge selection of fiction.

_____ 1. Invented by an American minister in 1869, *rickshaws* are now banned in many Asian cities.

_____ 2. In the summer, the sun *rises* too early for me.

_____ 3. Inés *spends* her summer vacations on the Greek island of Aegina.

_____ 4. The *musicians* brought their own music to the tryouts.

_____ 5. The average porcupine *has* more than thirty thousand quills.

EXERCISE 2   Identifying Verbs That Agree in Number with Their Subjects

For each sentence below, underline the subject of the sentence and the form of the verb in parentheses that agrees with the subject.

EX.   The <u>clouds</u> (*fill, fills*) the sky.

1. It is amazing that oysters (*create, creates*) beautiful pearls.

2. They (*join, joins*) the choir for the holiday pageant.

3. In the spring, trees (*sprout, sprouts*) leaves quickly when it rains.

4. The Humane Society (*has, have*) worked for decades to protect animals.

5. Some canned foods (*contain, contains*) no salt.

6   Every morning my little brother (*ask, asks*) for oatmeal.

7. In India, they (*serve, serves*) chicken biriyani on special occasions.

8. I (*like, likes*) fish for lunch.

9. You (*is, are*) what you eat.

10. Alicia's missing hamster (*run, runs*) out of the closet.

11. Eric (*make, makes*) a delicious salad with spinach and apples.

12. Tomorrow's championship game (*has, have*) been rescheduled.

13. Each volunteer (*promise, promises*) six hours of service.

14. Concerned parents (*is, are*) encouraging their children to wear sunscreen.

15. The candles (*glow, glows*) brightly in the darkened room.

INTERVENING PREPOSITIONAL PHRASES

8c   **The number of a subject is not changed by a phrase following the subject.**

EXAMPLES   The **winner** of those ribbons **is** the spaniel. [The verb *is* agrees with the subject *winner*.]

The seventh-grade **teacher**, along with a few of her students, **walks** to school. [The verb *walks* agrees with the subject *teacher*.]

Musicians from Peru and Ecuador **have** played in our auditorium. [The helping verb *have* agrees with the subject *Musicians*.]

EXERCISE 3   Identifying Verbs That Agree in Number with Their Subjects

In each of the following sentences, draw a line through the prepositional phrase or phrases between the subject and verb. Underline the subject. Then underline the verb in parentheses that agrees with the subject.

EX.   The <u>city</u> ~~of Amsterdam~~ (*has*, have) almost ninety islands.

1.   Children from all over the neighborhood (*wants, want*) to attend the birthday party.

2.   The library near the White House (*contains, contain*) more than twenty million books.

3.   Derrick's speech during the lunch period (*was, were*) heard down the hallway.

4.   The Statue of Liberty in Paris, like the one in New York City, (*stands, stand*) on an island.

5.   Loretta, along with her two friends, (*eats, eat*) tacos for lunch almost every day.

6.   Those books next to the window (*needs, need*) dusting.

7.   One of the wheels on my in-line skates (*sticks, stick*) when I skate.

8.   Sheila, but not her brother, (*is, are*) working tomorrow.

9.   The mountains in the distance (*belongs, belong*) to Italy.

10.   The gentleman with the red bow tie (*looks, look*) like my father.

EXERCISE 4   Proofreading Sentences for Subject-Verb Agreement

Most of the sentences below contain errors in subject-verb agreement. If a verb does not agree
with the subject, write the correct form of the verb on the line before the sentence. Write C if a
sentence is correct.

EX. _surrounds_   A large sheet of ice surround the South Pole.

_____   1. A continent of ancient forests are buried beneath the ice.

_____   2. Killer whales, along with leopard seals, lives in the Antarctic.

_____   3. The sea elephant, a good-natured creature, lie in the sun all day.

_____   4. These giants of the South Pole weighs a couple of tons.

_____   5. Sources of food are plentiful in the South Pole.

_____   6. The sea around the icecap is rich in fish and shrimp.

_____   7. Penguins at the South Pole lives in huge groups.

_____   8. Penguins, with their black and white feathers, resemble people in tuxedos.

_____   9. The killer whale, among the largest animals, grow to be as long as
                  twenty-seven feet.

_____   10. Many mysteries of the South Pole remains unsolved.

EXERCISE 5   Using Correct Subject-Verb Agreement

You are the manager of a toy store. You want to present your boss with a list of improvements
that could be made throughout the store. Think about comments that you have heard from the
customers about the toys, the employees, and the store itself. Then, write five of these comments
as complete sentences. Underline each subject once and each verb twice.

EX.   music too loud
       The music in the store is too loud.

1. _____

2. _____

3. _____

4. _____

5. _____

MODULE 8: AGREEMENT

SINGULAR AND PLURAL INDEFINITE PRONOUNS

Personal pronouns refer to specific people, places, things, or ideas. A pronoun that does not refer to a definite person, place, thing, or idea is called an ***indefinite pronoun***.

Personal Pronouns	I	we	you	it	he	she	they (singular)	them
Indefinite Pronouns	anyone	both	somebody	each	everyone			

Singular Indefinite Pronouns

8d   **The following indefinite pronouns are singular:** *each, either, neither, one, everyone, everybody, no one, nobody, anyone, anybody, someone, somebody.*

EXAMPLES   **Each** of the players **wears** a different hat.
             Does anybody have the correct time?

EXERCISE 6   Choosing Verbs That Agree in Number with Their Subjects

In each of the sentences below, underline the form of the verb in parentheses that agrees with the subject. Remember that the subject is never part of a prepositional phrase.

EX.   Nobody in my classes (*looks*, *look*) like that!

1. One of the firefighters (*have, has*) the frightened dog.

2. Everyone in the front row (*gets, get*) wet on that ride.

3. Don't take these lamps, because neither of them (*works, work*).

4. When I call that number, no one at your house (*answers, answer*).

5. Someone among the crowd of spectators always (*catches, catch*) those foul balls.

6. Each of the soldiers (*guards, guard*) a different door.

7. Somebody with good handwriting (*writes, write*) on the board.

8. Next time, everybody in both families (*gets, get*) a set of pictures.

9. Because those coins are gold, either of them (*is, are*) still valuable.

10. Anyone with scissors (*is, are*) able to learn origami.

Plural Indefinite Pronouns

8e   The following indefinite pronouns are plural: *both*, *few*, *many*, *several*.

EXAMPLES   **Few** of my friends **read** science fiction.
Many of them **like** science-fiction movies, though.

EXERCISE 7   Choosing Verbs That Agree in Number with Their Subjects

In each of the sentences below, underline the form of the verb in parentheses that agrees with the subject. Remember that the subject is never part of a prepositional phrase.

EX.   Both of the countries (*is*, <u>*are*</u>) in Central America.

1. Very few of the streets (*is*, *are*) wide enough for automobiles.

2. Many of the students (*has*, *have*) been to the science museum.

3. Several of the pictures (*is*, *are*) by Georgia O'Keeffe.

4. Few of the students in the contest (*has*, *have*) won a ribbon before.

5. Many of the newer kits (*is*, *are*) made of polyester film.

6. Several of the candidates (*want*, *wants*) to speak to you.

7. Both of the oil spills (*was*, *were*) finally cleaned up.

8. Several in my class (*has*, *have*) families in Mexico City.

9. Few of the workers (*knows*, *know*) when we will go to the new building.

10. Many of the blocks in the building (*was*, *were*) made of granite.

11. Few of these old books (*is*, *are*) still in print.

12. Many of the chairs (*match*, *matches*) this sofa.

13. Several of my friends (*attends*, *attend*) summer school.

14. Both of the notebooks (*belong*, *belongs*) to me.

15. (*Does*, *Do*) many of the students go home for lunch?

MODULE 8: AGREEMENT

ALL, ANY, MOST, NONE, *AND* SOME

8f **The indefinite pronouns *all*, *any*, *most*, *none*, and *some* may be either singular or plural.**

The number of the pronouns *all, any, most, none,* and *some* is determined by the number of the object in a prepositional phrase following the subject. If the pronoun refers to a singular object, it is singular. If the pronoun refers to a plural object, it is plural.

EXAMPLES   **Most** of the meal **is** cooked. [*Most* is singular because it refers to one thing—the *meal*. The verb *is* is singular to agree with the subject *Most*.]

        Most of the dishes are already washed. [*Most* is plural because it refers to more than one thing—*dishes*. The helping verb *are* is plural to agree with the subject *Most*.]

EXERCISE 8   Choosing Verbs That Agree in Number with Their Subjects

In each of the sentences below, underline the form of the verb in parentheses that agrees with the subject.

EX.   Some of the parks (*looks, look*) like gardens.

1. Most of the nearby cities (*offers, offer*) space for community gardens.

2. Some of my neighbors (*works, work*) on plots there.

3. All of my plot (*has, have*) sun most of the day.

4. Most of the families (*raises, raise*) food.

5. None of the parkland (*is, are*) wasted.

6. Some of the gardeners (*grows, grow*) flowers.

7. Today, all of the ground (*seems, seem*) to be covered with plants.

8. (*Do, Does*) any of these plants produce tomatoes?

9. Luckily, none of the plants (*needs, need*) extra care.

10. All of our tools (*helps, help*) us work quickly and easily.

EXERCISE 9   Proofreading Sentences for Subject-Verb Agreement

Many of the sentences below have errors in subject-verb agreement. Draw a line through each verb that does not agree with its subject. Write the correct verb form on the line before the sentence. Write *C* if the sentence is correct.

EX. __are__   None of the instruments is brass.

_____   1. Any of the songs sounds better on quality equipment.

_____   2. Most of the hall get too warm in July and August.

_____   3. None of the stage are used during our performance.

_____   4. Some of the piano is painted with black enamel.

_____   5. When it rains, all of the chairs stays dry under the canvas tent.

_____   6. All of the piccolos join in with the other woodwinds.

_____   7. Any of the music played on the flute are beautiful.

_____   8. None of the students wants to leave early.

_____   9. Most of the people likes summer concerts.

_____   10. Some of my friends is here from Germany.

EXERCISE 10   Choosing Verbs That Agree in Number with Their Subjects

For each sentence below, underline the verb form in parentheses that agrees with the subject.

EX. (*Does, Do*) any of those chairs seem ready to be painted?

1. All of your help at the harvest fair (*was, were*) appreciated.

2. Some of the clothes (*is, are*) dirty.

3. All of the actors (*plays, play*) more than one part.

4. Some of the water damage (*appears, appear*) on the ceiling.

5. None of the guests (*writes, write*) poetry.

REVIEW EXERCISE

A.   Identifying Verbs That Agree in Number with Their Subjects

For each sentence below, underline the verb form in parentheses that agrees with the subject.

EX.   One of Argentina's most popular dance forms (*is*, *are*) the tango.

1. Most of Argentina (*has, have*) a mild climate.

2. Most of the people in my class (*knows, know*) that the early Spanish explorers gave Argentina its name.

3. The Chaco, the north-central part of Argentina, (*produces, produce*) lumber.

4. One of the Chaco's most important trees (*is, are*) the quebracho tree.

5. Many of the people in Argentina (*vacations, vacation*) at the beach.

6. Several of the beaches (*extends, extend*) for miles.

7. Some of the swimmers (*enjoys, enjoy*) riding the waves in the surf.

8. Because there are lifeguards on the beach, everyone (*worries, worry*) less about safety.

9. Does everybody (*knows, know*) that Buenos Aires is the capital of Argentina?

10. Most of the southern tip of South America (*is, are*) occupied by Argentina.

B. Proofreading a Paragraph for Subject-Verb Agreement

In the following paragraph, draw a line through each verb that does not agree with its subject. In the space above each incorrect verb, write the correct form. If a verb is correct, write *C* above it.

cover
EX.   Mountains ~~covers~~ a large part of the earth.

[1] Many people throughout history has been attracted to mountaintops. [2] Some of the world's most famous landmarks is mountains. [3] One of the most beautiful mountains are Fujiyama in Japan. [4] Every summer, many men and women aim for the summit. [5] My aunt want to climb it next summer. [6] Also, everyone in Ito's family visit the top. [7] Most of the early climbers was men, because women were forbidden to climb the mountain until 1868. [8] The trip in the old days were difficult. [9] Now, however, several of the earlier problems no longer exists. [10] For example, today many of the climbers can buy food along the way instead of having to bring it.

MODULE 8: AGREEMENT
COMPOUND SUBJECTS

8g   **Subjects joined by *and* usually take a plural verb.**

EXAMPLE   **Justine and** her **brother like** to paint. [Two people like to paint.]

8h   **A compound subject that names only one person or thing takes a singular verb.**

EXAMPLE   **Macaroni and cheese is** my favorite dish. [One combination is meant.]

                Law and order is a major concern for the city. [One topic is a concern.]

EXERCISE 11   Identifying Verbs That Agree in Number with Their Subjects

For each sentence below, underline the correct form of the verb in parentheses.

     EX.   Photography and birds (*is*, <u>*are*</u>) two of my interests.

1. Josh and I (*wants*, *want*) to join the photography club at school.

2. My friend and his neighbor (*is*, *are*) giving a demonstration next week.

3. Mr. Tchong and his wife (*is*, *are*) both professional photographers.

4. Using digital cameras, he and she (*takes*, *take*) beautiful pictures of birds.

5. They recommend using a good telephoto lens because this (*is*, *are*) best for close-ups.

6. (*Does*, *Do*) Mr. Tchong and the students display their photographs at a gallery?

7. Mr. Tchong and his wife say that patience and practice (*is*, *are*) key to taking good photographs.

8. Locks and alarms (*is*, *are*) needed to protect expensive equipment.

9. During field trips, Lien and I (*watches*, *watch*) birds at the feeders.

10. A robin and her babies (*lives*, *live*) in a nearby tree.

8i   Singular subjects joined by *or* or *nor* take a singular verb. Plural subjects joined by *or* or *nor* take a plural verb.

EXAMPLES   **Neither Talasi nor** her **sister is** in my class. [Both subjects are singular.]

Either the **doctor or** the physician's **assistant is** available. [Both subjects are singular.]

Neither storms nor floods are forecast. [Both subjects are plural.]

Either buses or subways take you there. [Both subjects are plural.]

8j   When a singular subject and a plural subject are joined by *or* or *nor*, the verb agrees with the subject nearer the verb.

EXAMPLES   **Popcorn or** sunflower **seeds make** a good snack. [The verb agrees with the nearer subject, *seeds*.]

Sunflower **seeds or popcorn makes** a good snack. [The verb agrees with the nearer subject, *popcorn*.]

EXERCISE 12   Identifying Verbs That Agree in Number with Their Subjects

For each of the sentences below, underline the correct form of the verb in parentheses.

EX.   Either the artist or his assistant (*is*, *are*) shown in this picture.

1. Neither fruits nor vegetables (*was*, *were*) on the table.

2. Models or their props (*is*, *are*) sketched first.

3. Either the dishes or the cook (*was*, *were*) later added to the picture.

4. Neither Atul nor Cassie (*is*, *are*) responsible for that pastel.

5. Either a ticket or a pass (*allows*, *allow*) you to enter the museum.

6. (*Has*, *Have*) either Diego Rivera or Candido Partinari painted a mural in this city?

7. A camera or a sketchbook (*helps*, *help*) you remember the artwork.

8. Either the clerks or a guard (*has*, *have*) the correct time.

9. Neither our museum nor our galleries (*sells*, *sell*) that print.

10. Neither the catalog nor the bulletin board (*mentions*, *mention*) the museum.

COLLECTIVE NOUNS AND INVERTED SENTENCES

8k   **Collective nouns may be either singular or plural. A collective noun takes a singular verb when the noun refers to the group as a unit. A collective noun takes a plural verb when the noun refers to the individual parts or members of the group.**

A *collective noun* is singular in form but names a group of persons, animals, or things.

Common Collective Nouns			
audience	committee	group	swarm
class	family	herd	team
club	flock	jury	troop

EXAMPLES   The **team has** earned the award. [The team as a unit has earned the award.]

The **team have** arrived in separate cars. [Individual team members are in separate cars.]

8l   **When the subject follows the verb, find the subject and make sure that the verb agrees with it. The subject usually follows the verb in sentences beginning with *here* or *there* and in questions.**

EXAMPLES   Here **is** my **computer**.

There **are** new **programs** on the streaming service.

What **were** those **noises**?

Does lightning strike twice?

NOTE   When the subject of a sentence follows the verb, the word order is said to be *inverted*. To find the subject of a sentence with inverted order, restate the sentence in normal word order.

INVERTED   In the city **live** several famous **authors**.

RESTATED   Several famous **authors live** in the city.

INVERTED   **Were** the **Bennetts** with you?

RESTATED   The **Bennetts were** with you.

EXERCISE 13   Identifying Verbs That Agree in Number with Their Subjects

For each sentence below, underline the correct form of the verb in parentheses.

EX.   The committee (*was disagreeing*, <u>*were disagreeing*</u>) about the first speaker.

1. A flock of Canada geese (*lives, live*) in our city's park.
2. During the trial, the jury (*stays, stay*) at a nearby hotel.
3. Only one herd (*has appeared, have appeared*) at this water hole.
4. Now the majority (*is voting, are voting*) in the election.
5. The audience (*likes, like*) to applaud those actors.
6. The class (*perform, performs*) next weekend.
7. Visitors must be quiet when the Senate (*debates, debate*).
8. The squad (*does, do*) not agree with its captain.
9. That swarm of bees (*lives, live*) across the meadow.
10. The orchestra (*was, were*) magnificent.

EXERCISE 14   Identifying Verbs That Agree in Number with Their Subjects

Underline the subject in each of the sentences below. Then underline the correct form of the verb in parentheses.

EX.   There (*is*, <u>*are*</u>) many summer <u>holidays</u>.

1. There (*is, are*) a special day each June.
2. (*Is, Are*) the summer solstice here yet?
3. There (*is, are*) two solstices each year.
4. (*Was, Were*) the longest day of the year special?
5. Around the world, there (*is, are*) many celebrations on this day.
6. Here on the table (*lies, lie*) the key to the house.
7. Around eight o'clock, here (*comes, come*) my brothers.
8. (*Is, Are*) there any tomatoes left?
9. There (*is, are*) three reasons for doing that.
10. What (*is, are*) your excuse?

MODULE 8: AGREEMENT

AMOUNTS, TITLES, AND DON'T *AND* DOESN'T

Amounts and Titles

8m   **Words stating amounts are usually singular.**

A word or phrase stating a weight, a measurement, or an amount of money or time is usually considered one item. Such a word or phrase takes a singular verb.

EXAMPLES   **Ten grams is** a decagram.

                    Fifty cents is not much money today.

8n   **The title of a book or the name of an organization or a country, even when plural in form, usually takes a singular verb.**

EXAMPLES   *Black Folktales* **was written** by Julius Lester. [one book]

                    American Youth Hostels has headquarters in Washington, D.C. [one organization]

                    The **Sandwich Islands is** the old name for Hawaii. [one place]

EXERCISE 15   Identifying Verbs That Agree in Number with Their Subjects

In each of the following sentences, underline the correct form of the verb in parentheses.

EX.   The Friends of the Library (*has, have*) a book sale Saturday.

1. *Animal Fables from Aesop (is, are)* a book for readers of all ages.
2. Two hours sometimes (*seems, seem*) like a very long time.
3. The United States (*is, are*) full of public libraries.
4. (*Is, Are*) *Great Deeds of Superheroes* available in paperback?
5. Six feet (*is, are*) the average length of our tables.
6. One third plus two thirds (*equals, equal*) one.
7. Yes, *The ABC's of Stamp Collecting (has, have)* pictures of many colorful stamps.
8. The Canary Islands (*seems, seem*) like a good setting for a mystery.
9. Sixty-one dollars (*does, do*) seem like too much to pay.
10. On Monday, the Austin Volunteers for Neighborhood Libraries (*receives, receive*) donated books.

Don't and *Doesn't*

8o   ***Don't*** **and** *doesn't* **must agree with their subjects.**

The word *don't* is a contraction of *do not*, and *doesn't* is a contraction of *does not*. Use *don't* with all plural subjects and with the pronouns *I* and *you*.

EXAMPLES   The clouds **don't** look threatening.

I **don't** believe it!

You **don't** need a coat.

Use *doesn't* with all singular subjects except *I* and *you*.

EXAMPLES   The skateboard **doesn't** need paint.

She **doesn't** have kneeguards.

It **doesn't** work.

EXERCISE 16   Writing Original Sentences with *Don't* and *Doesn't*

You are taking two young cousins to the animal shelter where you volunteer. Your cousins are frightened by most animals, including dogs and cats. They are asking you lots of questions. You are trying to explain that they have nothing to fear. On the lines below, write five sentences about some of the animals. Explain why they are not to be feared or to be fed certain foods. Use *don't* and *doesn't* to agree with a different subject in each sentence.

EX.   We don't give cow milk to the kittens, Otis.
No, this dog doesn't want to be petted while it's eating.

1. _____

2. _____

3. _____

4. _____

5. _____

MODULE 8: AGREEMENT

PRONOUN-ANTECEDENT AGREEMENT

A pronoun usually refers to a noun or another pronoun called its *antecedent*.

8p   A pronoun agrees with its antecedent in number and gender.

Some singular personal pronouns have forms that indicate gender. Feminine pronouns refer to females. Masculine pronouns refer to males. Neuter pronouns refer to things (neither masculine nor feminine) and usually to animals.

Feminine	she	her	hers
Masculine	he	him	his
Neuter	it	it	its

EXAMPLES   Julie wondered if **she** would need **her** umbrella. [*She* and *her* are both feminine. They agree with the feminine antecedent *Julie*.]

Ruben asked if **his** friend could drop **him** at the corner. [*His* and *him* are both masculine. They agree with the masculine antecedent *Ruben*.]

The pan with the chili in **it** has lost **its** lid. [*It* and *its* are both neuter. They agree with *pan*, which is a thing.]

(1)   Use a singular pronoun to refer to *each, either, neither, one, everyone, everybody, no one, nobody, anyone, anybody, someone,* **or** *somebody.*

EXAMPLES   **Everyone** in the class took **her** or **his** project home. [*Her* and *his* are singular. Because *Everyone* may be either masculine or feminine, both forms are used.]

One of the exhibits lost **its** tag.

NOTE   Today it is acceptable to use the singular *they* to describe an unknown person. In addition, it is acceptable to use the pronoun *they* in a gender-neutral way to describe a known person who does not use gender-specific pronouns such as *he* or *she*.

EXAMPLES   **Everybody** brought **their** pets to the pet fair.

Sam is a student at the university. **They** are studying chemistry.

> **(2)** Use a singular pronoun to refer to two or more singular antecedents joined by *or*.
>
> EXAMPLES   Either my **mother or** my **aunt** will bring **her** map.
>
>   **Shane or Clay** will lend us **his** travel guide.
>
> **(3)** Use a plural pronoun to refer to two or more antecedents joined by *and*.
>
> EXAMPLES   **Lono and Nick** called **their** parents from the theater.
>
>   **Hanako and** her **friend** left early so that **they** could stop at the school.

EXERCISE 17   Identifying Antecedents and Writing Pronouns That Agree with Them

On the line in each sentence below, write a pronoun that will complete the meaning of the sentence. Then underline the antecedent, or antecedents, for that pronoun.

EX.   <u>Each</u> of the women in the audience waved <u>her</u> hand.

1. Kitty and Bruno worked together on _____ scenes.

2. Either Vern or Mr. Park will lend me _____ jacket.

3. One of the curtains is falling off _____ rod.

4. Vern and Kitty laughed at _____ lines in the first scene.

5. Dawn or Sabrena will bring _____ books from home.

6. Each of the actors should say _____ lines slowly and clearly.

7. Mrs. Park and my mother saved _____ programs from last year.

8. Anyone can try out if _____ enjoys acting.

9. Neither script has marks in _____ margins.

10. The actors took _____ bows in front of a cheering crowd.

MODULE REVIEW

A. Proofreading Sentences for Subject-Verb Agreement

Most of the sentences below contain agreement errors. For each error, draw a line through the incorrect verb. Write the correct form on the line before the sentence. Write *C* if the sentence is correct.

EX. <u>has</u>   Either the library or your teacher ~~have~~ the book.

_____ 1. Here is the photographs of sod houses.

_____ 2. The bricks of this house is made from grass-covered ground.

_____ 3. First, a man or a woman have to cut the prairie grass short.

_____ 4. Each person then dig out a strip of earth.

_____ 5. Where was those sod houses built?

_____ 6. *Sod House Memories* are about houses in Nebraska.

_____ 7. People in the United States don't build with sod much today.

_____ 8. Boards and bricks are available in most parts of the country.

_____ 9. Gene and Mai is working on a model of a sod house.

_____ 10. Paper bags or cloth are being used for windows.

B.   Proofreading a Paragraph for Pronoun-Antecedent Agreement

Find the errors in pronoun-antecedent agreement in the following paragraph. Draw a line through each pronoun that does not agree with its antecedent. In the space above the incorrect pronoun, write the correct form or write *C* if the sentence is correct.

               her
EX.   Neither Lacie nor Kathy gave ~~their~~ suggestions to Mr. Asari.

[1] Everyone was supposed to suggest ideas for how their class dues should be spent.

[2] Jodi and Brian wanted his money spent on a class trip. [3] Neither Isaac nor Theodore felt

that their idea was better. [4] Each of the aquariums needs a new hose for their air system.

[5] However, no one said that they wanted their money spent to replace the hoses. [6] Either Tom or Mario gave their suggestion next. [7] Both thought that his class should buy something permanent. [8] Jodi and Brian nodded their heads to this suggestion. [9] Each of the students voted for their choice. [10] Tom and Mario were happy to see that their idea pleased most of their classmates.

C. Writing About Animal Camouflage

You have been asked to conduct a class for the Environmental Club. Your topic will be how various animals protect themselves with camouflage.

1. First, do some research on animal camouflage. You might check encyclopedias, books about animals, and other reference books.
2. Find information about two kinds of camouflage, color matching and shape matching, and the animals that use them. Then write at least two sentences about each kind of camouflage. Be sure to use subject-verb agreement and pronoun-antecedent agreement.

color matching: _____

_____

_____

_____

shape matching: _____

_____

_____

_____

MODULE 9: USING VERBS CORRECTLY
PRINCIPAL PARTS OF VERBS

The four basic forms of a verb are called the ***principal parts***.

9a **The principal parts of a verb are the *present*, the *present participle*, the *past*, and the *past participle*.**

Present	Present Participle	Past	Past Participle
walk	(is) walking	walked	(have) walked
make	(is) making	made	(have) made

Notice that the present participle and the past participle require helping or auxiliary verbs (forms of *be* and *have*).

The principal parts of a verb are used to express whether the action of the verb takes place in present, past, or future time.

PRESENT He **makes** homemade bread.

He **is making** a loaf of bread now.

PAST Yesterday they **made** rye bread.

They **have** often **made** bread together

FUTURE Tomorrow we **will make** more bread.

By next week, we **will have made** many more loaves.

Because *walk* forms its past and past participle by adding *-ed*, it is called a ***regular verb***. *Make* forms its past and past participle differently, so it is called an ***irregular verb***.

EXERCISE 1   Identifying the Time Expressed by Verbs

For each sentence below, study the verb form in italics. Look for other words that give clues about the time the verb expresses. On the line before each sentence, write *PR* if the action takes place in the present, *PA* if the action takes place in the past, or *F* if the action takes place in the future.

EX. __past__   We *have visited* our cousins in Puerto Rico many times.

_____ 1. You *are talking* too softly for us to understand your words.

_____ 2. I *heard* a great joke yesterday.

_____ 3. My family *lived* in Philadelphia for three years.

_____ 4. Pete *asked* Felicia for a ride to last night's drama club meeting.

_____ 5. Doty *is driving* to her guitar lesson in her new car.

_____ 6. I *will make* your lunch in a few minutes.

_____ 7. He *will need* a new coat in the fall.

_____ 8. Abdul *has* already *left* for the movies.

_____ 9. Please hurry, for they *are waiting* for us.

_____ 10. We *will sell* tickets for the band concert next Wednesday at the mall.

EXERCISE 2   Identifying the Principal Parts of Verbs

On each line below, identify the principle part of the verb form shown. Write *PR* for *present*, *PRP* for *present participle*, *PA* for *past*, or *PAP* for *past participle*.

EX. ___PRP___ (is) playing

_____ 1. sing   _____ 6. (has) started

_____ 2. (is) trying   _____ 7. helped

_____ 3. judged   _____ 8. (have) believed

_____ 4. (are) working   _____ 9. looked

_____ 5. clean   _____ 10. believe

REGULAR VERBS

9b   A *regular verb* forms its past and past participle by adding *-ed* or *-d* to the present form.

Present	Present Participle	Past	Past Participle
wish	(is) wishing	wished	(have) wished
hop	(is) hopping	hopped	(have) hopped
happen	(is) happening	happened	(have) happened
move	(is) moving	moved	(have) moved

EXERCISE 3   Writing the Forms of Regular Verbs

The present form is given for each of the following verbs. Fill in the chart with the present participle, past, and past participle of each verb.

Present	Present Participle	Past	Past Participle
EX. wish	(is) wishing	wished	(have) wished
1. look	(is)		(have)
2. select	(is)		(have)
3. shop	(is)		(have)
4. use	(is)		(have)
5. start	(is)		(have)

EXERCISE 4   Writing Sentences with Forms of Regular Verbs

Write a sentence using the correct form of each italicized verb below.

EX.   past of *cal*   I called the jewelry store.

1. present participle of *hope* _____

_____

2. past participle of *enjoy* _____

_____

3. past of *drop* _____

_____

4. past participle of *raise* _____

_____

5. present participle of *slip* _____

_____

6. past participle of *talk* _____

_____

7. past of *ask* _____

_____

8. present participle of *answer* _____

_____

9. past of *follow* _____

_____

10. present participle of *laugh* _____

_____

MODULE 9: USING VERBS CORRECTLY

IRREGULAR VERBS

9c An *irregular verb* forms its past and past participle in some other way than by adding *-d* or *-ed* to the present form.

If you are not sure about the principal parts of a verb, look in a dictionary. An entry for an irregular verb lists the principal parts of the verb. If the principal parts are not given in the dictionary entry, the verb is a regular verb.

COMMON IRREGULAR VERBS			
Present	**Present Participle**	**Past**	**Past Participle**
begin	(is) beginning	began	(have) begun
bite	(is) biting	bit	(have) bitten *or* bit
blow	(is) blowing	blew	(have) blown
break	(is) breaking	broke	(have) broken
bring	(is) bringing	brought	(have) brought
build	(is) building	built	(have) built
burst	(is) bursting	burst	(have) burst
catch	(is) catching	caught	(have) caught
choose	(is) choosing	chose	(have) chosen
come	(is) coming	came	(have) come
cost	(is) costing	cost	(have) cost
do	(is) doing	did	(have) done
draw	(is) drawing	drew	(have) drawn
drink	(is) drinking	drank	(have) drunk
drive	(is) driving	drove	(have) driven
eat	(is) eating	ate	(have) eaten
fall	(is) falling	fell	(have) fallen
feel	(is) feeling	felt	(have) felt
freeze	(is) freezing	froze	(have) frozen
get	(is) getting	got	(have) gotten *or* got

COMMON IRREGULAR VERBS			
Present	Present Participle	Past	Past Participle
give	(is) giving	gave	(have) given
go	(is) going	went	(have) gone
grow	(is) growing	grew	(have) grown
hurt	(is) hurting	hurt	(have) hurt
know	(is) knowing	knew	(have) known
lead	(is) leading	led	(have) led
lend	(is) lending	lent	(have) lent
lose	(is) losing	lost	(have) lost
make	(is) making	made	(have) made
meet	(is) meeting	met	(have) met
put	(is) putting	put	(have) put
ride	(is) riding	rode	(have) ridden
ring	(is) ringing	rang	(have) rung
run	(is) running	ran	(have) run
say	(is) saying	said	(have) said
see	(is) seeing	saw	(have) seen
sell	(is) selling	sold	(have) sold
send	(is) sending	sent	(have) sent
shrink	(is) shrinking	shrank *or* shrunk	(have) shrunk *or* shrunken
sing	(is) singing	sang	(have) sung
sink	(is) sinking	sank *or* sunk	(have) sunk *or* sunken
speak	(is) speaking	spoke	(have) spoken
stand	(is) standing	stood	(have) stood
steal	(is) stealing	stole	(have) stolen
swim	(is) swimming	swam	(have) swum
take	(is) taking	took	(have) taken
tell	(is) telling	told	(have) told
throw	(is) throwing	threw	(have) thrown
wear	(is) wearing	wore	(have) worn
win	(is) winning	won	(have) won
write	(is) writing	wrote	(have) written

EXERCISE 5   Writing the Forms of Irregular Verbs

On the line in each of the following sentences, write the correct form (past or past participle) of the verb shown in italics.

EX.   *tell*   Reggie <u>told</u> us about the work of the naturalist John Muir.

1. *write*   Reggie and Ed have _____ a play.

2. *win*   As student playwrights, they have _____ many awards.

3. *put*   Last year, they _____ on a play about John Muir's life.

4. *make*   In his books and articles, John Muir _____ many people aware of the beauty of the wilderness.

5. *know*   Even a hundred years ago, Muir _____ that the wilderness was endangered.

6. *choose*   He _____ to write about the wilderness in an effort to save it.

7. *come*   Also, through his efforts, the Sierra Club _____ into being.

8. *grow*   Muir _____ up on a farm in Wisconsin.

9. *get*   He _____ his education at the University of Wisconsin.

10. *lead*   His studies of plants _____ him to explore the woods for wildflowers.

11. *begin*   John Muir _____ his wilderness journeys as a young man.

12. *go*   He _____ on foot from Kentucky to Florida, collecting plants.

13. *write*   As he walked, he _____ in his journals about the plants he saw.

14. *give*   These journals have _____ many readers a guide to wildflowers.

15. *send*   Muir's studies eventually _____ him to California.

16. *see*   In California, he _____ the Yosemite Valley.

17. *say*   In his writings, he _____ that this valley is one of the United States' greatest treasures.

18. *draw*   The beauty of the valley has _____ many visitors over the years.

19. *build*   People _____ a dam to collect water in a huge lake there.

20. *take*   Many hikers have _____ the path that leads to Bridalveil Fall.

EXERCISE 6   Using Past and Past Participle Forms of Irregular Verbs to Write Interview Questions

A group of athletes has come to your school to train for the Olympics. You have been selected to interview the athletes. Your assignment is to find out facts about their backgrounds, training, skills, and hopes for winning gold medals. Write ten questions that you might ask these athletes. In your questions, use the past or past participle forms of at least ten verbs. Underline each verb (including any helping verbs) that you use.

EX.   Why <u>have</u> you <u>chosen</u> to compete in the Olympics?

1. _____

   _____

2. _____

   _____

3. _____

   _____

4. _____

   _____

5. _____

   _____

6. _____

   _____

7. _____

   _____

8. _____

   _____

9. _____

   _____

10. _____

   _____

TENSE

9d **The *tense* of a verb indicates the time of the action or of the state of being expressed by the verb.**

Every verb has six tenses.

Tenses	Examples
Present	I see, you see, she sees
Past	I saw, we saw, they saw
Future	I will (shall) see, you will see, he will see
Present Perfect	I have seen, you have seen, she has seen
Past Perfect	I had seen, you had seen, he had seen
Future Perfect	I will (shall) have seen, she will have seen, they will have seen

This time line shows the relationship between the six tenses.

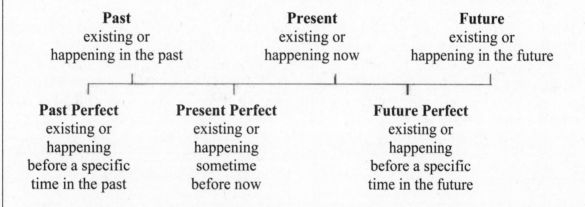

9e **Do not change needlessly from one tense to another.**

When writing about events that take place in the present, use verbs that are in the present tense. When writing about events that occurred in the past, use verbs that are in the past tense.

INCONSISTENT	As we **walk** through the park, we **met** Latrice.
	[*Walk* is in the present tense, and *met* is in the past tense.]
CONSISTENT	As we **walk** through the park, we **meet** Latrice.
	[Both *walk* and *meet* are in the present tense.]
CONSISTENT	As we **walked** through the park, we **met** Latrice.
	[Both *walked* and *met* are in the past tense.]

EXERCISE 7   Revising a Paragraph to Make Tenses of the Verbs Consistent

Many of the verbs in the paragraph below are inconsistent in tense. Rewrite the paragraph on the lines below. Change the verb forms to make their tenses consistent.

EX.   We climbed the hill, and I see storm clouds.

We climbed the hill, and I saw storm clouds.

[1] Odessa, Benny, and I are on a hike in the woods, and we got lost. [2] We start up a steep hill. [3] "Oh, no!" I shouted. [4] From the top of the hill, I see storm clouds. [5] A bad storm was rushing toward us. [6] Looking for cover, we run down the hill. [7] Then Benny finds a small cave in the side of the hill. [8] We climb in under the big rocks just as the rain started falling. [9] Rain falls for about an hour. [10] During that time, we cheer each other up with jokes and waited for the storm to pass.

_____

_____

_____

_____

_____

_____

_____

_____

_____

_____

_____

SIT *AND* SET *AND* RISE *AND* RAISE

Sit and *Set*

9f   The verb *sit* means "to be seated" or "to rest." *Sit* seldom takes an object. The verb *set* means "to place" or "to put (something)." *Set* usually takes an object. Unlike *sit*, *set* has the same form for the present form, past, and past participle.

Present	Present Participle	Past	Past Participle
sit	(is) sitting	sat	(have) sat
set	(is) setting	set	(have) set

EXAMPLES   Melita and I **sat** in the back of the room. [no object]

Bobby Ray **set** the package on the table. [Bobby Ray set what? *Package* is the object.]

Wilbur, my German shepherd, **is sitting** on the couch. [no object]

Jonah **is setting** his luggage on the cart. [Jonah is setting what? *Luggage* is the object.]

EXERCISE 8   Writing the Forms of *Sit* and *Set*

On the line in each of the sentences below, write the correct form of *sit* or *set*.

EX.   Last night I <u>sat</u> in the kitchen and wrote a letter.

1. Elmore _____ the chairs around the table.

2. Come _____ by the fire and talk to me.

3. The cat is _____ on the new rug in the den.

4. _____ your rake down and rest for a while.

5. The chess players have _____ at their game tables all morning.

Rise and Raise

9g The verb *rise* means "to move upward" or "to get up." *Rise* almost never takes an object. The verb *raise* means "to lift (something) up." *Raise* usually takes an object.

Present Form	Present Participle	Past	Past Participle
rise	(is) rising	rose	(have) risen
raise	(is) raising	raised	(have) raised

EXAMPLES   The sun **rose** at six o'clock this morning. [no object]

Franco **raised** his hand. [Franco raised what? *Hand* is the object.]

According to the report, the price of wheat **will rise** next year. [no object]

Melba **will raise** the curtain now. [Melba will raise what? *Curtain* is the object.]

EXERCISE 9 Identifying the Correct Forms of *Rise* and *Raise*

For each of the sentences below, underline the correct form of *rise* or *raise* in parentheses.

EX.   Everyone was silent as Iola (*rose, raised*) from her seat.

1. Should I (*rise, raise*) my voice so you can hear me more clearly?

2. We like to watch the drawbridge (*rise, raise*).

3. She explained that last summer she had (*rose, raised*) the price of her flowers.

4. Two weeks after she planted the seeds, little plants (*rose, raised*) from the ground.

5. As the heat was (*rising, raising*) during the summer, she watered the plants twice a day.

MODULE 9: USING VERBS CORRECTLY

LIE *AND* LAY

9h The verb *lie* means "to recline," "to be in place," or "to remain lying down." *Lie* never takes an object. The verb *lay* means "to put (something) down" or "to place (something)." *Lay* usually takes an object.

Present	Present Participle	Past	Past Participle
lie	(is) lying	lay	(have) lain
lay	(is) laying	laid	(have) laid

EXAMPLES The dog **is lying** in the sun. [no object]
Janos **is laying** the plates on the table. [Janos is laying what? *Plates* is the object.]

Last night, **I lay** in bed and thought about our picnic. [no object]
Before class, I **laid** the book on the desk. [I laid what? *Book* is the object.]

EXERCISE 10   Identifying the Correct Forms of *Lie* and *Lay*

For each of the sentences below, underline the correct form of *lie* or *lay* in parentheses.

EX.   The Delaware River (*lies*, *lays*) on the western border of New Jersey.

1. Last night, we (*lay*, *laid*) our sleeping bags in the back of the van.
2. You kids can (*lie*, *lay*) there and nap during our long trip to New Jersey.
3. Don't forget your phone with the GPS app, which is (*lying*, *laying*) on the kitchen table.
4. Oh, no! I think the beach towels (*lay*, *laid*) in the washer all night.
5. (*Lie*, *Lay*) them over the kitchen chairs so that they will be dry before we leave.

EXERCISE 11   Writing the Forms of *Lie* and *Lay*

Complete each of the sentences below by filling in the blank with the correct form of *lie* or *lay*.

EX.   After the storm yesterday, deep puddles of water <u>lay</u> in the driveway.

1. Please _____ your papers on my desk.

2. My sweater was covered with dog hair after the dog had _____ on it.

3. Hans had _____ your library books on the table in the hall.

4. Did you find the empty bowl that was _____ on the shelf?

5. Morris had _____ the garden tools somewhere in the garage.

6. Vietnam _____ on the eastern coast of mainland Southeast Asia.

7. Maria has already _____ compost on the new garden.

8. We had _____ on the beach too long in the hot sun.

9. _____ the tablecloth on the table while I get the plates and glasses.

10. Workers are _____ a new surface on the northbound side of Route 95.

EXERCISE 12   Proofreading for the Correct Forms of *Lie* and *Lay*

Most of the sentences below contain errors in the use of *lie* and *lay*. If a sentence contains the wrong verb form, write the correct form on the line before the sentence. If a sentence is correct, write *C* on the line before it.

EX.   <u>lying</u>   Empty soda cans were laying all over the field after the concert.

_____ 1. Do horses lay down to rest?

_____ 2. Before bed, he lay more wood on the fire.

_____ 3. Ernest was lying on the couch, reading the newspaper.

_____ 4. Barbara has lain the puzzle pieces out on the card table.

_____ 5. When he finished reading, Parvis lay his book on the shelf.

MODULE REVIEW

A. Identifying the Correct Forms of *Sit* and *Set, Rise* and *Raise,* and *Lie* and *Lay*

For each of the sentences below, underline the correct form of the verb in parentheses.

> EX.   When the man asked who wanted the extra tickets, I (*rose, raised*) my hand.

1. We were (*sitting, setting*) in the front row at the concert.
2. The lights dimmed as a platform (*rose, raised*) from beneath the stage.
3. Workers had (*sat, set*) that platform beneath a hidden trapdoor.
4. On the platform, they had (*lain, laid*) a red carpet, and on the carpet they had (*set, sat*) a couple of stools.
5. Even with the lights dimmed, we could see that someone was (*sitting, setting*) on one of the stools.
6. Suddenly, the lights (*rose, raised*) to full power.
7. Then Linda (*rose, raised*) her head and smiled.
8. A microphone was (*lying, laying*) on the stool beside her.
9. She began to sing as she (*sat, set*) there.
10. The audience (*rose, raised*) from their seats to join her as she sang "The Star-Spangled Banner."

B. Proofreading a Paragraph for Correct Verb Forms

Most of the sentences in the following paragraph contain incorrect verb forms. If a sentence contains an error, draw a line through the wrong form of the verb. Write the correct form above the verb. Write *C* above sentences in which the verb forms are correct.

> grew
> EX.   Ann Petry ~~growed~~ up in Connecticut.

[1] Ann Petry goed to college at the University of Connecticut. [2] After graduating from

college, she begun her career as a pharmacist. [3] Later, she selled advertisements for a

newspaper. [4] Eventually, she raised to the position of newspaper reporter. [5] Her newspaper

career leads her to write novels and short stories. [6] She has wrote many novels and nonfiction

books. [7] As she wrote those works, she used her own experiences and interests as background.

[8] *The Street* telled a story about life in a Harlem neighborhood. [9] *Harriet Tubman:*

Conductor on the Underground Railroad gave readers valuable information about slavery in the

United States. [10] Petry's books have became very popular with readers all over the world.

C.   Using Regular and Irregular Verbs to Write a Letter

Choose an interesting place anywhere in the world that you would like to visit. Go online to gather information about the place. What interesting sights might you see there? What historical events might you learn about during your visit? Imagine you got to visit this place, and write a letter to tell a friend at home about your trip. In your letter, describe some of the sights that you have seen so far. Use at least five regular verbs and five irregular verbs in your letter. Proofread your finished letter for correct use of verb tenses. Underline the verbs that you use.

EX. Dear Taja,
  I <u>visited</u> the Galapagos Islands yesterday! I <u>saw</u> an extremely old tortoise.

_____
_____
_____
_____
_____
_____
_____
_____
_____
_____
_____
_____
_____
_____
_____
_____
_____
_____

10a *Case* is the form of a noun or pronoun that shows how it is used. There are three cases: *nominative*, *objective*, and *possessive*.

The form of a noun is the same for the nominative and the objective cases.

NOMINATIVE CASE   The **teacher** asked a question. [noun used as subject]

OBJECTIVE CASE   Bianca answered the **teacher**. [noun used as a direct object]

A noun changes its form only in the possessive case, usually by adding an apostrophe and an *s*.

POSSESSIVE CASE   The **teacher's** question was about geography.

Unlike nouns, most personal pronouns have different forms for the nominative, objective, and possessive cases.

PERSONAL PRONOUNS		
Singular		
Nominative Case	**Objective Case**	**Possessive Case**
I	me	my, mine
you	you	your, yours
he, she, it, (they)	him, her, it, (them)	his, her, hers, its, (their, theirs)
Plural		
Nominative Case	**Objective Case**	**Possessive Case**
we	us	our, ours
you	you	your, yours
they	them	their, theirs

NOTES   Some teachers prefer to call possessive forms of pronouns (such as *our*, *your*, and *their*) adjectives. Follow your teacher's instructions regarding possessive forms.

Today it is acceptable for writers or speakers to use the pronoun *they* in a gender-neutral way to describe a known person who does not use gender-specific pronouns such as *he* or *she*. In addition, the singular *they* is used in informal speech to describe an unknown person and is also accepted in formal writing.

EXAMPLES   Someone just left the restaurant and *they* left their phone on the table. (unknown person)

Addy is a freshman in high school. *They* like soccer and working on the school newspaper. (known person)

EXERCISE 1   Identifying Personal Pronoun Forms

Identify the case of each italicized pronoun in the following sentences. On the line before each sentence, write *N* for *nominative*, *O* for *objective*, and *P* for *possessive*.

EX. __O__ I showed *him* the mural on the school wall.

_____ 1. *My* mother carves wooden animals.

_____ 2. Did *you* read about the baseball player Hank Aaron?

_____ 3. The teacher told *us* to write two haiku poems each.

_____ 4. Sonya and *I* painted the doghouse purple.

_____ 5. It was *our* idea to have an international food festival.

_____ 6. Phillis Wheatley was one of the first African American poets to have *her* poems published.

_____ 7. That book is *his* to take home and study.

_____ 8. *They* wanted to start a school newspaper.

_____ 9. Did Antonio give *you* a tour of his home?

_____ 10. The watercolor painting in the hall is *mine*.

NOMINATIVE CASE PRONOUNS

10b   The subject of a verb is in the nominative case.

A subject tells *whom* or *what* the sentence is about.

EXAMPLES   **We** have a parakeet named Pícaro. [*We* is the subject of *have*.]

It is a beautiful bird. [*It* is the subject of *is*.]

She and **I** taught Pícaro to speak. [*She* and *I* are used together as the compound subject of *taught*.]

To help you choose the correct pronoun in a compound subject, try each form of the pronoun separately.

EXAMPLE   My brother and (*I, me*) like Pícaro.

I like Pícaro.

Me like Pícaro.

ANSWER   My brother and **I** like Pícaro.

EXAMPLE   (*He, Him*) and (*I, me*) played with Pícaro.
He played with Pícaro.
Him played with Pícaro.
I played with Pícaro.
Me played with Pícaro.

ANSWER   **He** and **I** played with Pícaro.

10c   A predicate nominative is in the nominative case.

A ***predicate nominative*** follows a linking verb and identifies or explains the subject of the verb. A pronoun used as a predicate nominative usually identifies the subject and follows a form of the verb *be* (such as *am, are, is, was, were, be, been,* or *being*).

EXAMPLES   The winner of the contest was **he.** [*He* follows the linking verb *was* and identifies the subject *winner*.]

The winners should have been **she** and **I.** [*She* and *I* follow the linking verb *should have been* and identify the subject *winners*.]

NOTE   In informal, everyday conversation, people often use forms such as *It's me* and *That was her*. However, these forms are not standard, formal English.

EXERCISE 2   Choosing Pronouns Used as Subjects

In each sentence below, underline the pronoun or pair of pronouns that completes the sentence correctly.

EX.   Roberto and (_she_, her) collect stamps.

1. Yesterday, Roberto and (*me, I*) got together with our stamp albums.
2. For an hour or so, (*we, us*) traded stamps.
3. Then (*him and me, he and I*) read the advertisements in the latest issues of *Stamp Collecting* and *Stamp Digest*.
4. (*They, Them*) are two magazines for stamp collectors.
5. (*He, Him*) saw an advertisement for unusual stamps from Angola.

EXERCISE 3   Proofreading Sentences for Correct Use of Nominative Case Pronouns

Check each sentence carefully. If a sentence below contains the wrong form of a pronoun, write the correct form on the line before the sentence. If a sentence contains no errors, write *C* on the line.

EX. __he__   The person who wrote that poem might have been him.

_____ 1. Are your favorite poets Langston Hughes and her?
_____ 2. It was she who wrote the poem "Metaphor."
_____ 3. The best poets in our class are him and I.
_____ 4. The poems included in our program should have been them.
_____ 5. Among the poets in this book are Dorothy Parker and he.

10d   *Direct objects* and *indirect objects* of verbs are in the objective case.

A *direct object* follows an action verb and tells *whom* or *what* receives the action of the verb.

EXAMPLES   Mrs. Delaney called **me** last night. [*Me* tells *whom* Mrs. Delaney called.]

Sam returned **them** to the library. [*Them* tells *what* Sam returned to the library.]

An *indirect object* comes between an action verb and a direct object. It tells *to whom* or *to what* or *for whom* or *for what* the action is done.

EXAMPLES   The plants are dry; I'll give **them** some water. [*Them* tells *to what* I'll give water. *Water,* the direct object, tells *what* I'll give.]

Dr. Irwin bought **us** the tickets. [*Us* tells *for whom* Dr. Irwin bought the tickets. *Tickets,* the direct object, tells *what* he bought.]

To choose the correct pronoun in a compound object, try each form of the pronoun separately in the sentence.

EXAMPLE   Bob invited Heta and (*she, her*). [*Bob invited she. Bob invited her.*]

ANSWER   Bob invited Heta and **her**.

EXERCISE 4   Writing Pronouns Used as Direct Objects and Indirect Objects

Complete each sentence below by writing an appropriate pronoun on the line in the sentence. Use a variety of pronouns, but do not use *you* or *it*.

EX.   I met Ossie and <u>her</u> at the movies last night.

1. Karina wants you to call _____ as soon as possible.
2. We think you should give _____ another chance.
3. Gina loaned _____ a pencil because I didn't have one.
4. Daniel just got here. Tell _____ that joke you heard last night.
5. Our team beat _____ in the tournament.

EXERCISE 5   Identifying Correct Pronoun Forms

Each sentence below contains two pronouns in parentheses. Complete each sentence by underlining the correct pronoun.

EX.   The mayor gave (*we, us*) an award.

1. The city council nominated Rafael and (*I, me*) because we worked hard all summer to clean up the vacant lot.
2. Other students helped (*we, us*), too.
3. When the workers were finished, the boss presented (*they, them*) with a letter from the city.
4. Turning the lot into a park helped the city and (*we, us*).
5. People in the neighborhood loaned Melba and (*she, her*) rakes and brooms.

EXERCISE 6   Proofreading Sentences for Correct Use of Pronouns

If a sentence below contains an incorrect pronoun, draw a line through the pronoun and then write the correct pronoun on the line before the sentence. If the sentence contains no pronoun errors, write *C* on the line.

EX. __me__   Aunt Lois joined Tina and I at the auditorium.

_____ 1. Mr. Tamaka chose her and Philippe for the leading roles in the play.
_____ 2. The director called Sue and they for another audition.
_____ 3. Tina told Phoebe and I about the rehearsal schedule.
_____ 4. On Tuesday, my mother drove me to the rehearsal.
_____ 5. The dancers in the play gave Symon and she flowers after the performance.

MODULE 10: USING PRONOUNS CORRECTLY

PRONOUNS AS OBJECTS OF PREPOSITIONS

10e   The *object of a preposition* is in the objective case.

A *prepositional phrase* is a group of words consisting of a preposition, a noun or a pronoun that serves as the object of the preposition, and any modifiers of that object.

EXAMPLES   June waved at **us**. [*Us* is the object of the preposition *at*.]

The letter was addressed to **her** and **me**. [*Her* and *me* are the compound object of the preposition *to*.]

EXERCISE 7   Choosing Correct Pronouns Used as Objects of Prepositions

Complete each sentence below by underlining the correct pronoun or pair of pronouns in parentheses.

EX.   The food was shared by (*he and she, him and her*).

1. Please pass the enchiladas to (*me, I*).
2. Enchiladas are rolled tortillas that have cheese or some other filling in (*they, them*).
3. Aunt Sofia gave this recipe for enchiladas to my brother and (*I, me*).
4. It is the best recipe for (*we, us*).
5. After softening the tortillas, put meat, cheese, or another filling in (*they, them*).
6. Roll up the tortillas and put grated cheese on top of (*they, them*).
7. Listen to (*him and I, him and me*) talk about the cooking directions.
8. Why don't you stay and eat dinner with (*us, we*)?
9. Just between you and (*I, me*), this will be one of the best meals you've ever tasted.
10. According to (*him, he*), we should eat enchiladas every day of the week.

EXERCISE 8   Using Pronouns as Objects of Prepositions

Each sentence below contains a noun or a phrase in italics. On the line before each sentence, write a pronoun that could be used to replace the italicized word or words.

EX. _them_   Hillary sent postcards to *Wanda and Sue*.

_____ 1. An interesting man sat between my *sister and me* on the airplane.

_____ 2. My sister stayed close to *Mom and Dad* as we walked through the airport.

_____ 3. This was an exciting but scary experience for *my sister*.

_____ 4. The steward on the plane gave snacks to *all the passengers*.

_____ 5. In spite of *the crying baby*, we had a good flight.

_____ 6. For *Dad*, this would be a business trip.

_____ 7. While Dad worked, we stayed with *Aunt Isobelle* in Amsterdam.

_____ 8. Aunt Isobelle toured the canals along with *my sister and me*.

_____ 9. Everyone toured the house where Anne Frank had lived except *Aunt Isobelle*.

_____ 10. Then we went to see paintings by *Vincent van Gogh* at a local museum.

WHO *AND* WHOM

10f **The pronoun *who* has different forms in the nominative and objective cases. *Who* is the nominative form. *Whom* is the objective form.**

NOTE   In spoken English, the use of *whom* is becoming less common. In fact, when you are speaking, you may correctly begin any question with *who* regardless of the grammar of the sentence. In written English, however, you should distinguish between *who* and *whom*.

When you need to decide whether to use *who* or *whom* in a question, follow these steps:

Step 1:   Rephrase the question as a statement.
Step 2:   If you can replace the word with *he*, *she*, or *they*, use *who*. If you can replace the word with *him*, *her*, or *them*, use *whom*.

EXAMPLE   *(Who, Whom) are those men?*
Step 1:   The statement is *Those men are (who, whom)*.
Step 2:   If you can replace the word with *he*, *she*, or *they*, use *who*. If you can replace the word with *him*, *her*, or *them*, use *whom*.

*Those men are **they**.* CORRECT
*Those men are **them**.* INCORRECT

ANSWER   **Who** are those men?

EXERCISE 9   Choosing *Who* or *Whom*

In each sentence below, underline the correct pronoun form.

EX.   (*Who, Whom*) did he choose?

1. (*Who, Whom*) is your coach?
2. The winners of the game were (*who, whom*)?
3. To (*who, whom*) did you loan my book?
4. (*Who, Whom*) have we forgotten to put on the list?
5. (*Who, Whom*) did you sit beside in math class?
6. (*Who, Whom*) is the present for?
7. For (*who, whom*) did you make that burrito?
8. In the fourth quarter, he passed the ball to (*who, whom*)?
9. With (*who, whom*) will you share your orange?
10. (*Who, Whom*) is your science teacher?

EXERCISE 10   Proofreading for Errors in the Use of *Who* and *Whom*

If a sentence below contains an error in the use of *who* or *whom,* write the correct pronoun on the line before the sentence. If a sentence contains no errors, write *C* on the line.

EX. ___Whom___   Who have you invited to the party?

_____ 1. Who called while I was in the shower?

_____ 2. Whom will get your vote for class president?

_____ 3. For who did Zeinab design that costume?

_____ 4. With whom are we going to the movies?

_____ 5. Whom wants another carrot stick?

MODULE 10: USING PRONOUNS CORRECTLY

PRONOUN APPOSITIVES AND REFLEXIVE PRONOUNS

PRONOUNS AS APPOSITIVES

Sometimes a pronoun is followed directly by a noun that identifies the pronoun. Such a noun is called an *appositive*.

EXAMPLE   We **students** held a car wash. [The noun *students* is an appositive identifying the pronoun *we*.]

10g   **In deciding which pronoun to use before an appositive, omit the appositive, and try each form of the pronoun separately.**

EXAMPLE   Last night, (*we, us*) musicians had a concert. [*We had a concert. Us had a concert.*]

ANSWER   Last night, **we** musicians had a concert.

EXAMPLE   The police officer thanked (*we, us*) volunteers. [*The police officer thanked we. The police officer thanked us.*]

ANSWER   The police officer thanked **us** volunteers.

EXERCISE 11 Choosing Correct Pronouns for Appositives

Complete each sentence below by filling in the blank with either the pronoun *we* or the pronoun *us*.

EX.   That was an exciting game for <u>us</u> Cardinals.

1. _____ pet owners should take our animals to the veterinarian for regular checkups.

2. The store gave _____ clerks a large raise in our hourly pay.

3. Yesterday _____ Orioles fans were disappointed at the outcome of the game.

4. Sadly, _____ farmers have had very little rain for our crops this year.

5. Who will design the costumes for _____ chorus members?

REFLEXIVE PRONOUNS

A *reflexive pronoun* refers to the subject and directs the action of the verb back to the subject.

REFLEXIVE PRONOUNS	
First Person	myself, ourselves
Second Person	yourself, yourselves
Third Person	himself, herself, itself, themselves

10h **The reflexive pronouns *himself* and *themselves* can be used as objects. Don't use the nonstandard forms *hisself* and *theirselfs* or *theirselves* in place of *himself* and *themselves*.**

INCORRECT The farmer made hisself a shed for his tractor.

CORRECT The farmer made **himself** a shed for his tractor.

INCORRECT Of course, most candidates vote for theirselves.

CORRECT Of course, most candidates vote for **themselves**.

EXERCISE 12   Identifying Correct Pronoun Forms

For each of the sentences below, underline the correct pronoun in parentheses.

EX.   They helped (*themselves, theirselves*) to the lemonade.

1. Ansel Adams really enjoyed (*hisself, himself*) while taking pictures.
2. People who gossip should keep their words to (*themselves, theirselves*).
3. Virgil and his friends often keep to (*theirselves, themselves*) and rarely come to our meetings.
4. While preparing for the test, Elton asked (*hisself, himself*) many review questions.
5. All by (*himself, hisself*), John built a playhouse for his little brother.

MODULE 10: USING PRONOUNS CORRECTLY
MODULE REVIEW

A. Identifying Correct Pronoun Forms

For each of the sentences below, underline the correct pronoun in parentheses.

EX.   Frank sent Gina and (*she, her*) a letter.

1. Craig St. Clair and (*he, him*) have become very successful high school coaches.
2. They told (*theirselves, themselves*) not to be afraid on the roller coaster.
3. (*Who, Whom*) have you told about your experience in Milan?
4. The librarian was very helpful to Samantha and (*me, I*).
5. (*We, Us*) volunteers are always happy to help out in an emergency.

B. Correcting Errors in Pronoun Use

Most sentences in the paragraph below contain at least one error each in the use of pronoun forms. Correct each pronoun error by drawing a line through it and writing the correct pronoun form above it. Write *C* above each sentence that is correct.

EX.   For ~~we~~ us athletes, Kenny Walker is an inspiration.

[1] As a young child, Kenny Walker set a goal for hisself. [2] He would not let being deaf stop him from achieving his dreams. [3] At school the other children and him played games at recess. [4] Because Kenny was deaf, the team captains often picked he last. [5] To they, Kenny was someone who might not have the skills to play. [6] However, Kenny and his mother told theirselves not to give up. [7] Between him and she, they made a promise to work and train. [8] By the time his friends and him were in high school, Kenny was a great football player. [9] He went on to the University of Nebraska, where he became the defensive player of the year in the Big Eight. [10] Whom was Kenny after college? [11] He was a defensive end for the Denver Broncos. [12] To us football fans, his story is one of courage and strength.

[13] Every time he ran out onto the playing field, Kenny Walker taught an important lesson to you and I. [14] Us players should always keep that lesson in mind. [15] People can often succeed even when them are challenged. [16] It seems to me that every person has problems and challenges special to him or she. [17] Each of us people must work hard to deal with those problems and challenges. [18] Kenny Walker believed in hisself. [19] He showed you and I that dreams can come true if a person is willing to work hard. [20] My favorite player is him, Kenny Walker.

11a The three degrees of comparison of modifiers—adjectives and adverbs—are the *positive*, the *comparative*, and the *superlative*.

(1) The *positive degree* is used when only one thing is being described.

EXAMPLES   The water is **cold**.
Brad swam **swiftly** to shore.

(2) The *comparative degree* is used when two things are being compared.

EXAMPLES   This water is **colder** than the water in Florida.
Tanya swam **more swiftly** than the girl in the next pool lane.

(3) The *superlative degree* is used when three or more things are being compared.

EXAMPLES   The water in Maine is the **coldest** of any water I've found.
Of all the racers, Brad swam the **most swiftly**.

REGULAR COMPARISON

Most one-syllable modifiers form their comparative and superlative degrees by adding -*er* and -*est*. Notice that both adjectives and adverbs form their degrees of comparison in the same way.

Positive	Comparative	Superlative
warm	warmer	warmest
thin	thinner	thinnest
straight	straighter	straightest
fast	faster	fastest

Some two-syllable modifiers form their comparative and superlative degrees by adding -*er* and -*est*. Other two-syllable modifiers form their higher degrees of comparison using *more* or *most*. To show a lower degree of comparison, modifiers form the comparative degree by using *less* and the superlative degree by using *least*.

Positive	Comparative	Superlative
funny	funnier	funniest
tiny	tinier	tiniest
cheerful	more cheerful	most cheerful
often	more often	most often
sneaky	less sneaky	least sneaky
extreme	less extreme	least extreme

Modifiers that have three or more syllables form the comparative degree by using *more* or *less* and the superlative degree by using *most* or *least*.

Positive	Comparative	Superlative
difficult	less difficult	least difficult
important	more important	most important
thoughtfully	less thoughtfully	least thoughtfully
mysteriously	more mysteriously	most mysteriously

EXERCISE 1 Forming Degrees of Comparison of Modifiers

On the lines provided, write the forms for the comparative and superlative degrees of each of the following modifiers. Use a dictionary as necessary.

EX.   sharp   sharper/less sharp   sharpest/least sharp

1. costly   _____   _____

2. independent   _____   _____

3. wise   _____   _____

4. lightly   _____   _____

5. beautiful   _____   _____

6. hungry   _____   _____

7. cautiously   _____   _____

8. hopeful   _____   _____

9. proud   _____   _____

10. shyly   _____   _____

11b **Some modifiers form their comparative and superlative forms in other ways.**

Positive	Comparative	Superlative
bad	worse	worst
far	farther	farthest
good	better	best
well	better	best
many	more	most

EXERCISE 2   Writing Comparative and Superlative Forms of Modifiers

On the line before each of the sentences below, write the correct form of the modifier in parentheses. Use a dictionary as necessary.

EX. __best__   Aunt Eliana makes the (*good*) enchiladas I have ever tasted.

_____ 1. Jeremy swam (*far*) than any of the other boys.

_____ 2. Joe has collected (*many*) sports cards than Tim.

_____ 3. In the state swimming meet, Kelly performed (*well*) than she ever had before.

_____ 4. Yori is (*good*) in math than in spelling.

_____ 5. The country with the (*many*) people is China.

_____ 6. The flooding is threatening to become (*bad*) than last month's flooding.

_____ 7. Neptune is the (*far*) planet from the sun.

_____ 8. This is the (*much*) money I have ever saved!

_____ 9. Hurricane Irma was one of the (*bad*) storms to hit Florida in recent times.

_____ 10. After taking medicine for three days, he felt (*well*) than he had in two weeks.

EXERCISE 3   Using Comparative and Superlative Forms of Modifiers

In the blanks in the following paragraph, write appropriate modifiers of the words *good*, *many*, and *well*.

EX.   The <u>worst</u> act in the variety show was the one with the dancing poodles.

[1] Yesterday, we went to see a really _____ show at the Grayson theater. [2] It was a variety show with _____ funny, quirky, unusual acts. [3] Perhaps the _____ bizarre of all the acts was the guy who played "The Battle Hymn of the Republic" by banging on a lot of plumbing fixtures. I enjoyed the folk singer from Chile. [4] She sang really _____. However, my favorite act was the gospel singer. [5] Hers was the _____ performance of the evening.

EXERCISE 4   Writing Sentences with Correct Forms of Modifiers

You are a movie reviewer. Think about your favorite or least favorite movies and their plots, characters, actors, and endings. In your review, write five complete sentences that form the higher and lower degree of comparisons by using the comparative and superlative forms of modifiers. Put two lines under the comparative and superlative degrees of modifiers.

EX.   The <u>funniest</u> movie I have ever seen is *Home Alone*. Macaulay Culkin is <u>quicker</u> than the crooks and <u>better</u> than they are at setting traps.

_____

_____

_____

_____

_____

_____

_____

_____

_____

_____

_____

SPECIAL PROBLEMS IN USING MODIFIERS

11c   Use *good* to modify a noun or a pronoun. Use *well* to modify a verb.

EXAMPLES   Julio enjoys reading a **good** mystery story. [*Good* modifies the noun *story*.]

The dinner that you made was a **good** one. [*Good* modifies the pronoun *one*.]

His broken leg is healing **well**. [*Well* modifies the verb phrase *is healing*.]

Good should not be used to modify a verb.

INCORRECT   Lydia speaks Spanish good.

CORRECT   Lydia speaks Spanish **well**.

11d   Use adjectives, not adverbs, after linking verbs.

A linking verb such as *look*, *feel*, and *become*, is often followed by a predicate adjective. The adjective modifies the subject.

EXAMPLE   Kadeem looked **nervous** on stage. [The predicate adjective *nervous* modifies the subject *Kadeem*.]

NOTE   Some linking verbs can also be used as action verbs. As action verbs, they may be modified by adverbs.

EXAMPLE   Tegan looked **wistfully** at the new computers. [*Wistfully* modifies the action verb *looked*.]

EXERCISE 5   Using Adjectives and Adverbs Correctly

On the line before each sentence, write the correct adjective or adverb from the pair in parentheses.

EX.   <u> sad </u>   Jerry felt (*sad*, *sadly*) about losing the race.

_____ 1. Cynthia had a fever and didn't look (*good*, *well*).

_____ 2. The flowers grew (*quick*, *quickly*) in the garden.

_____ 3. If you like scary movies, you will think that this is a (*good*, *well*) one.

_____ 4. Please stay (*quiet, quietly*) during the play.
_____ 5. That camera takes (*good, well*) pictures.
_____ 6. The tortillas smell (*fresh, freshly*).
_____ 7. That plant will not grow (*strong, strongly*) without water and sun.
_____ 8. The band practiced all week and sounds (*well, good*) now.
_____ 9. Rebecca writes poetry (*good, well*).
_____ 10. The dog smells his food (*careful, carefully*) before eating it.

EXERCISE 6   Finding and Correcting Misused Modifiers in a Paragraph

In the paragraph below, there are ten misused modifiers. Draw a line through each mistake and write the correct form above it.

surely
EX.   I ~~sure~~ enjoyed the movie.

[1] I could tell that summer was coming quick. [2] And I am happily that it is almost

summer. [3] According to the weather forecaster, it will be a well summer with lots of sun.

[4] When I go to the beach this summer, I have to be carefully that I do not get a sunburn.

[5] The cold water at the beach feels well on a hot day. [6] I always run into the waves and get

wet quick. [7] Some of my friends ease in slow. [8] If the wind blows good, we fly a kite at the

water's edge. [9] Sometimes I walk along the high-water mark and look close for interesting

shells or stones. [10] I know I will feel sadly when summer is over.

DOUBLE COMPARISONS

11e   Avoid double comparisons.

A *double comparison* is the use of both *-er* and *more* (less) or *-est* and *most* (least) to form a comparison. When you make a comparison, use only one form, not both.

INCORRECT   Dad's old car had a more smoother ride than his new one has.

CORRECT   Dad's old car had a **smoother** ride than his new one has.

INCORRECT   This is the most quickest way to the airport.

CORRECT   This is the **quickest** way to the airport.

11f   Avoid the use of double negatives.

A *double negative* is the use of two negative words to express one negative idea.

Common Negative Words			
barely	never	none	nothing
hardly	no	no one	nowhere
neither	nobody	not (-n't)	scarcely

INCORRECT   Shing didn't have none of his allowance left.

CORRECT   Shing had **none** of his allowance left.

INCORRECT   She couldn't find a seat nowhere else on the train.

CORRECT   She could find a seat **nowhere** else on the train.

CORRECT   She could**n't** find a seat anywhere else on the train.

EXERCISE 7   Eliminating Double Comparisons and Double Negatives

Revise the following sentences to eliminate the double comparisons and double negatives.

EX.   Math seems more easier this year than last year.
      <u>Math seems easier this year than last year.</u>

1. Jon had not never been out of the country. _____

    _____

2. Penny won't never forget her best friend. _____

    _____

3. Traffic is most heaviest around five o'clock in the afternoon. _____

_____

4. Ted isn't going to the meeting neither. _____

_____

5. The baby was more quieter than a mouse. _____

_____

6. Are you working more longer than you used to? _____

_____

7. I am not doing nothing tonight. _____

_____

8. Hasn't James never seen the ocean? _____

_____

9. Dominique couldn't never be mean to anyone. _____

_____

10. Of all the members of the basketball team, Antonio is the most shortest. _____

_____

EXERCISE 8   Revising to Correct Double Comparisons and Double Negatives

Rewrite the paragraph below, correcting nonstandard use of modifiers.

EX.   The Mbuti live in the Congo region in one of the world's most richest forests.
       The Mbuti live in the Congo region in one of the world's richest forests.

[1] The Mbuti don't use nothing but leaves and branches to build a village. [2] A woman starts building a hut by making a dome from the more younger trees in a clearing. [3] Leaves cover this dome, keeping out the most worst rain and winds. [4] The Mbuti never live hardly more than two months in one place. [5] They move on to make a new village where food sources are more closer.

_____

_____

_____

_____

_____

_____

PLACEMENT OF MODIFIERS

11g   **Place modifying phrases and clauses as close as possible to the words they modify.**

Notice how the meaning of these sentences changes when the position of the phrase *across the street* changes.

EXAMPLES   The woman **across the street** opened a clothing shop for children. [The phrase modifies *woman*.]
The woman opened a clothing shop for children **across the street.** [The phrase modifies *children*.]
Across the street, the woman opened a clothing shop for children. [The phrase modifies *opened*.]

A ***prepositional phrase*** is a group of words consisting of a preposition, a noun or pronoun that serves as the object of the preposition, and any modifiers of that object. A prepositional phrase used as an adjective should be placed directly after the word it modifies.

MISPLACED   The dog ran up to Julie **with long, shaggy hair**.

CLEAR   The dog **with long, shaggy hair** ran up to Julie.

A prepositional phrase used as an adverb should be placed near the word it modifies.

MISPLACED   Janet read about a lost kitten **in that magazine**.

CLEAR   **In that magazine**, Janet read about a lost kitten.

Avoid placing a prepositional phrase so that it seems to modify either of two words. Place the phrase so that it clearly modifies the word you intend it to modify.

MISPLACED   Rico said **on Friday** he had found a missing wallet. [Does the phrase modify *said* or *found*?]

CLEAR   Rico said that he had found a missing wallet **on Friday**.

CLEAR   **On Friday**, Rico said that he had found a missing wallet.

EXERCISE 9   Revising Sentences with Misplaced Prepositional Phrases

The meaning of each of the following sentences is not clear because the modifying phrase is misplaced. Decide where the phrase belongs. Then write the revised sentence on the line.

EX.   Willis gave a speech to explain how to look for a job at the new civic center.
<u>Willis gave a speech at the new civic center to explain how to look for a job.</u>

1. The girl is jogging around the park from next door. _____

_____

2. The boy was riding on a bicycle in blue polka-dot shorts. _____

_____

3. She gave the gift to the boy with the pink wrapping paper. _____

_____

4. I heard a report that a bad storm is coming on the radio. _____

_____

5. The train arrived after we had lunch from San Diego. _____

_____

EXERCISE 10   Placing Prepositional Phrases Correctly

Rewrite each of the following sentences by adding the prepositional phrase given in parentheses. Be careful to place each prepositional phrase near the word or words it modifies.

EX.   Many paintings show strange, fantastical scenes. (by Marc Chagall)
Many paintings by Marc Chagall show strange, fantastical scenes.

1. Elaine put the shirt on the baby. (*with green stripes*)

_____

2. The monkey was chattering at the children. (*in the tree*)

_____

3. The girl is making a dress. (*with pigtails*)

_____

4. We learned that a big blizzard was coming. (*from Aunt Melanie*)

_____

5. The boy was walking the dog. (*with the red boots*)

_____

PLACEMENT OF PARTICIPIAL PHRASES AND ADJECTIVE CLAUSES

11h A *participial phrase* consists of a verb form—either a present participle or a past participle—and its related words. A participial phrase modifies a noun or a pronoun. Like a prepositional phrase, a participial phrase should be placed as close as possible to the word that it modifies.

EXAMPLES   **Listening to the radio**, she heard her favorite song. [The participial phrase modifies *she*.]

                Greg's violin, **bought at a secondhand store**, is actually a valuable antique. [The participial phrase modifies *violin*.]

A participial phrase that is not placed next to the noun or pronoun that it modifies is a *misplaced modifier*.

MISPLACED   Lying on the back seat of the car, Jon found his guitar.

    CLEAR   Jon found his guitar **lying on the back seat of the car**.

A participial phrase that does not clearly and sensibly modify a word in the sentence is a *dangling participle.*

DANGLING   Visiting the city's animal shelter, the perfect puppy was found.

    CLEAR   **Visiting the city's animal shelter**, we found the perfect puppy.

11i An *adjective clause* modifies a noun or a pronoun. Most adjective clauses begin with a relative pronoun—*that, which, who, whom,* or *whose.*

MISPLACED   My Uncle Len works for a paint company who is trying to grow a beard.

    CLEAR   My Uncle Len, **who is trying to grow a beard**, works for a paint company.

EXERCISE 11   Revising Sentences to Correct Errors in the Use of Modifiers

On the lines below, revise the sentences to correct the errors in the placement of modifiers. [Hint: You will need to add, delete, or rearrange some words.]

EX.   The band began to play for the huge audience marching down the football field.
      <u>Marching down the football field, the band began to play for the huge audience.</u>

1. Deirdre has earned a scholarship whose record is outstanding. _____

   _____

2. Listening to the words, tears suddenly came to my eyes. _____

   _____

3. The dress does not fit me that you made. _____

   _____

4. Played by the band, I heard some of my favorite songs. _____

   _____

5. The man hurried through the store wearing a raincoat and boots. _____

   _____

6. The teacher saw two owls camping at the river. _____

   _____

7. Sitting under that shady tree, some of my best poems are written. _____

   _____

8. We saw a herd of deer driving along the freeway. _____

   _____

9. The Battle of Saratoga saved the American Revolution which was fought in 1777. _____

   _____

10. I found a book at the library that was written by Amy Tan. _____

   _____

MODULE 11: USING MODIFIERS CORRECTLY
MODULE REVIEW

A.   Correcting Misplaced and Dangling Modifiers

Each of the following sentences contains a dangling or misplaced modifier. On the lines after each sentence, rewrite the sentence so that it is clear and correct.

> EX.   The car was driven by the man with new paint and white sidewall tires.
> <u>The man drove the car with new paint and white sidewall tires.</u>

1. He told us that he had saved his allowance for a year to buy the bike at the party.

    _____

    _____

2. Hurtling through space, some scientists think asteroids will someday hit the earth.

    _____

    _____

3. Driving to the mall, a shortcut was discovered.

    _____

    _____

4. An orange lay on the table that had been peeled.

    _____

    _____

5. I got a dog from the pet shop that is only six weeks old.

    _____

    _____

B. Identifying and Correcting Errors in the Use of Modifiers

Rewrite the following paragraph to eliminate the errors in the use of modifiers.

EX.   There aren't hardly any tigers left in one of India's national parks.
        There are hardly any tigers left in one of India's national parks.

[1] Some people believe that tigers are the most beautifulest of all the animals. [2] In the past, tourists who wanted to see tigers couldn't find no better place than this park. [3] The tigers here seemed more friendlier. [4] The chances to see a tiger here were well. [5] This situation was due to the fact that the tigers were protected so good by the park system. [6] Today, though, you can't scarcely find a tiger in the park. [7] In 1991, the larger number of tigers counted was forty-five. [8] In 1992, the count was smallest; there were only seventeen tigers left. [9] Much tigers have been killed by poachers. [10] Other tigers may have grown tiredly of having humans around, and so they may have left the park.

MODULE 12: A GLOSSARY OF USAGE

ACCEPT / AS (LIKE)

The lessons on the next few pages contain a *glossary*, or alphabetical list, of common problems in English usage. You will notice that a number of examples used in this glossary are labeled *standard* or *nonstandard*. **Standard English** is used in *formal* situations, such as speeches and assignments for school. It is also used in *informal* situations, such as conversations and everyday writing. **Nonstandard English** does not follow the rules and guidelines of standard English.

accept, except   *Accept* is a verb that means "to receive." *Except* may be either a verb or a preposition. As a verb, it means "to leave out." As a preposition, it means "excluding."

EXAMPLES   Theo **accepted** the award. [verb]

Because she is not feeling well, Meredith will be **excepted** from play rehearsal. [verb]

Everyone **except** Sienna attended the concert. [preposition]

ain't   Avoid this word in speaking and writing. It is nonstandard English. Use *is not, am not*, or *are not*.

all right   Used as an adjective, *all right* means "satisfactory" or "unhurt." Used as an adverb, *all right* means "well enough." *All right* should always be written as two words. (*Alright* is nonstandard English.)

EXAMPLES   The weather looks **all right** for a picnic. [adjective]

Rosie did **all right** in the spelling contest. [adverb]

a lot   *A lot* should always be written as two words.

EXAMPLE   There is **a lot** of food left over from Jon's birthday party.

already, all ready   *Already* means "previously." *All ready* means "completely prepared."

EXAMPLES   Everyone in our group was **already** on the bus by the time Mr. Lo arrived.

I practiced for a long time, and I'm **all ready** for my piano recital tonight.

Among   See *between, among*.

As   See *like, as*.

EXERCISE 1   Identifying Correct Usage

In the following sentences, underline the correct word or words in parentheses.

EX.   All the boys are in line (*accept*, *except*) Michael.

1. Zara (*accepted*, *excepted*) the nomination to become student council president.
2. Seth had a bad cold, but he's (*all right*, *alright*) now.
3. Suzi is packed and (*already*, *all ready*) to visit her aunt in Austin.
4. Because of the large crowd, there (*ain't*, *aren't*) many empty seats.
5. No school council members will be (*accepted*, *excepted*) from today's meeting.
6. By the time the waitress brought Rico's lasagna, I had (*already*, *all ready*) finished eating my lunch.
7. The store sold every copy of Amy Tan's latest book (*accept*, *except*) one.
8. Because I don't have to do (*alot*, *a lot*) of homework, I can go to the concert with you.
9. Did August (*accept*, *except*) the nomination for class officer?
10. Theresa read (*alot*, *a lot*) of Mariana's poems.

between, among   Use *between* when referring to two people or things at a time. They may be part of a group consisting of more than two. Use *among* when referring to a group rather than to separate individuals. Typically, *among* is used when referring to more than two persons or things; *between* is typically used when referring to only two.

EXAMPLES   I divided the work **between** Abdul and Jamie.

There isn't much difference **between** these two brands of soap.

The job of preparing and printing the programs was divided **among** six students. [The six students are thought of as a group.]

bring, take   *Bring* shows action directed *toward* the speaker or writer. *Take* shows action directed *away from* the speaker or writer. Think of *bring* as related to *come* and *take* as related to *go.*

EXAMPLES   **Bring** the microphone to me.

Please **take** the piano stool with you.

bust, busted   Avoid using these words in place of *burst* or *break.*

EXAMPLES   A balloon **bursts** when stuck with a pin [not *busts*]

His glasses **broke** when he dropped them. [not *busted*]

could of   Do not use *of* with the helping verb *could.* Use *have* instead. Also avoid *ought to of, should of, would of, might of,* and *must of.*

EXAMPLE   Tito's band could **have** performed all night. [not *of*]

except   See *accept, except.*

fewer, less   *Fewer* is used with plural words. *Less* is used with singular words. *Fewer* tells "how many," and *less* tells "how much."

EXAMPLES   Samantha told **fewer** jokes than she had planned.

There was **less** applause last night.

good, well   *Good* is always an adjective. Never use *good* to modify a verb; use *well,* which is an adverb.

INCORRECT   Marjorie and Paco sang their duet good.

CORRECT   Marjorie and Paco sang their duet **well.**

NOTE	*Feel good* and *feel well* mean different things. *Feel good* means "to feel happy or pleased." *Feel well* means "to feel healthy."
	EXAMPLES Performing makes me feel **good**.
	After eating the large meal, Paula did not feel **well**.

had ought, hadn't ought   Do not use *had* with the word *ought*.

INCORRECT   The director had ought to give clearer directions to the cast.

CORRECT   The director **ought** to give clearer directions to the cast.

EXERCISE 2   Revising Sentences by Correcting Errors in Usage

The sentences below contain errors in usage. Draw a line through each mistake and write the correction above it. Revise each sentence using standard English. [Note: A sentence may contain more than one error.]

EX.   No one wanted to try the soup ~~accept~~ Willard. *(except written above)*

1. Mark would of come to the show, but he caught the flu and doesn't feel good.

2. As I was getting into my costume, the zipper busted.

3. David hadn't ought to lift that piece of stage scenery by himself.

4. Will you take the magician's rabbit over here to us?

5. Mrs. Adriana divided the pizza between the six of us.

6. Sam felt well because he had less tests on Tuesday than Paula did.

7. I wish I could of brought the dog on our trip.

8. I have less sponsors than you for the Walk for Hunger.

9. You had ought to clean your room before Mom gets home.

10. He busted out laughing when I told him the joke I had just heard.

hisself, theirself, theirselves   These words are nonstandard English. Use *himself* and *themselves*.

EXAMPLES   Yoshi was proud of **himself** for finishing the race. [not *hisself*]

The girls gave **themselves** extra time to study. [not *theirselves*]

its, it's   *Its* is a personal pronoun in the possessive case. *It's* is a contraction of *it is* and *it has*.

EXAMPLES   Please feed the cat because **it's** ready for **its** dinner. [*It's* is the contraction of *it is*. *Its* is a possessive pronoun.]

It's been snowing since yesterday [*It's* is the contraction of *it has*.]

kind, sort, type   The words *this, that, these,* and *those* should agree in number with the words *kind, sort,* and *type. This* and *that* are singular. *These* and *those* are plural.

EXAMPLES   **That kind** of bird is rarely seen in this part of the country.

Those kinds of cars are very reliable.

learn, teach   *Learn* means "to acquire knowledge." *Teach* means "to instruct" or "to show how."

EXAMPLES   Danielle is **learning** how to play chess.

Mr. Haddad is **teaching** Jayden how to play the guitar.

less   See *fewer, less*.

like, as   *Like* is a preposition; therefore, it introduces a prepositional phrase. In informal English, *like* is often used as a conjunction meaning "as." In formal English, *as* is always preferred.

EXAMPLES   **Like** my mother, I order sushi when we go out to eat. [*Like* introduces the phrase *Like my mother*.]

Shahla added one cup of milk, **as** the recipe directed. [*As the recipe directed* is a clause and needs the conjunction *as*, not the preposition *like*, to introduce it.]

might of, must of   See *could of*.

real In informal English, the adjective *real* is often used as an adverb meaning "very" or "extremely." In formal English, use an adverb such as *very* or *extremely* if a more descriptive adjective is not available.

> INCORRECT   Their new house is real bright because of the large windows.
>
> CORRECT   Their new house is **quite** bright because of the large windows.

this here, that there The words *here* and *there* are not needed after *this* and *that*.

> EXAMPLES   Mia can ride **this** horse. [not *this here*]
>
> **That** one might be too playful for her. [not *that there*]

try and In informal English, *try and* is often used for *try to*. In formal English, *try to* is preferred.

> INCORRECT   Let's try and win a prize.
>
> CORRECT   Let's **try to** win a prize.

EXERCISE 3   Revising Sentences by Correcting Errors in Usage

The sentences below contain twenty errors in usage. Draw a line through each mistake and write the correction above it. Revise each sentence using standard English.

> as
> EX.   The young children weren't acting ~~like~~ they should have.

1. Will you learn me how to cook these fresh vegetables, Mrs. Rodríguez?

2. They must of looked at pictures of theirselves in the photo album no less than ten times.

3. Saburo tried and taught hisself some magic tricks real quickly.

4. Should we try and finish our report by this here Wednesday?

5. Sabrina might of decided to study piano like her brother did.

6. That there wolf taught it's cubs to hunt for theirself.

7. Its too bad; your cousin might of won.

8. These sort of hand-woven rugs are imported real often from around the world.

well   See *good, well*.

when, where   When writing a definition, do not use *when* incorrectly.

INCORRECT   "Occasional" is when something happens now and then.

CORRECT   "Occasional" means something happens now and then.

where   Do not use *where* for *that*.

EXAMPLE   I read on a map **that** two of the countries bordering China are India and Mongolia. [not *where*]

who, which, that   The relative pronoun *who* refers to people only. *Which* refers to things only. *That* refers to things or to classes of people.

EXAMPLES   Li is the student **who** is collecting money for the field trip. [person]

Here are the concert tickets, **which** were a gift from my aunt. [things]

The waiter brought me the empanada **that** I ordered. [thing]

This school attracts the kind of people **that** enjoy volunteering. [class of people]

whose, who's   *Whose* is the possessive form of *who*. *Who's* is a contraction of *who is* or *who has*.

EXAMPLES   **Whose** jacket is on the floor? [possessive pronoun]

Who's at the door? [contraction of *who is*]

Who's finished reading the module? [contraction of *who has*]

without, unless   Do not use the preposition *without* in place of the conjunction *unless*.

EXAMPLE   Don't use your computer **unless** Paul first shows you how. [not *without*]

would of   See *could of*.

your, you're   *Your* is the possessive form of *you*. *You're* is a contraction of *you are*.

EXAMPLES   **Your** brother answered the phone.

You're just in time for dinner.

EXERCISE 4   Identifying Correct Usage

In the following sentences, underline the correct word or words in parentheses.

EX.   (*Whose*, <u>*Who's*</u>) been to Ellis Island in New York?

1. Myrtilla Miner was the person (*who, which*) opened an African American girls' school in Washington, D.C., in 1851.
2. I believe (*your, you're*) sitting in my seat.
3. A synonym is (*a word that, when a word*) has the same or nearly the same meaning as another word.
4. Did you forget (*your, you're*) jacket on the bus?
5. Sara was the first person (*who, which*) answered the phone.
6. There is the boy (*whose, who's*) pen I borrowed.
7. I read in our textbook (*that, where*) February 5, 1917, is the date the Mexican constitution was enacted.
8. The bus driver won't leave (*unless, without*) all the students are seated.
9. From this far away, Sabrina can't see (*good, well*) without her glasses.
10. (*Who's, Whose*) going to have some of these *buñuelos* with me?

EXERCISE 5   Using Words Correctly

Write a sentence that correctly uses any five of the glossary entries below.

well (good)	without, unless
when, where	would of (could of)
who, which, that	your, you're
whose, who's	

EX.   Did she give you your books?

1. _____

_____

2. _____

_____

3. _____

_____

4. _____

_____

5. _____

_____

MODULE 12: A GLOSSARY OF USAGE
MODULE REVIEW

A.   Identifying Correct Usage

In the following sentences, underline the correct word or words in parentheses.

EX.   Marian Anderson was (*between, among*) this country's greatest opera singers.

1. I read (*that, where*) a famous conductor said Ms. Anderson had the kind of voice that is heard only "once in a hundred years."

2. Because she was African American, Marian Anderson was not always (*accepted, excepted*) by audiences of the 1920s and 1930s.

3. By that time, she was (*already, all ready*) a well-known singer.

4. In 1939, the Daughters of the American Revolution decided that Marian Anderson (*hadn't ought to, shouldn't*) sing in Constitution Hall.

5. Eleanor Roosevelt, (*who, which*) was First Lady, found Ms. Anderson a place to sing.

6. She didn't want anything to stop Ms. Anderson from coming to Washington, D.C., to (*bring, take*) her music to the people.

7. Try (*and, to*) imagine what it was like on that cold afternoon at the Lincoln Memorial.

8. Ms. Anderson must (*of, have*) been amazed to see seventy-five thousand people in the audience.

9. She sang (*a lot, alot*) of beautiful songs.

10. Marian Anderson, (*whose, who's*) voice thrilled audiences everywhere, died in 1993.

B.   Revising Sentences to Correct Errors in Usage

Some of the following sentences contain errors in usage. Rewrite each sentence correctly in the spaces below. If a sentence is correct, write *C* after its number.

EX.   I'd like to buy this ~~here~~ belt.

1. Melissa is a shy person who doesn't like alot of attention.

   _____

2. During the extremely cold weather, our water pipes froze, and then they busted.

   _____

3. Will Anna be at the sports banquet to except her trophy?

   _____

4. Please bring me a glass of water.

   _____

5. They sold less tickets to the play than they had hoped.

   _____

6. Those type of watches are no longer being made.

   _____

7. Salvador tried to wipe hisself off after falling in the mud.

   _____

8. With her head tucked into her green jacket, the little girl looked like a turtle.

   _____

9. I can't believe that your moving so far away.

   _____

10. Mrs. Olivero should of told us that we were having a surprise quiz today.

   _____

MODULE 13: CAPITAL LETTERS

THE PRONOUN I AND PROPER NOUNS

13a   Capitalize the pronoun *I*.

EXAMPLE   Perhaps **I** can help you.

13b   Capitalize proper nouns.

A ***proper noun*** is a specific name for a particular person, place, thing, or idea. It is always capitalized. A ***common noun*** names a type of person, place, thing, or idea. A common noun is not capitalized unless it begins a sentence or is part of a title.

Proper Nouns	Common Nouns
Brazil	country
August	month
Santha Rama Rau	author
Sequoia National Park	park
USS *Nautilus*	submarine

Some proper nouns consist of more than one word. In these names, prepositions and articles (*a, an,* and *the*) are not capitalized.

EXAMPLES   Declaration **of** Independence
Eric **the** Red

EXERCISE 1   Identifying Correct Capitalization

For each of the following pairs of phrases, write *C* on the line before the phrase that is capitalized correctly.

   EX. _____   a.   visit a Museum
      _*C*_   b.   visit the Museum of Science

_____ 1. a. in late September
              b. in late september
_____ 2. a. the Empire State Building
              b. a Building in New York City
_____ 3. a. my parents and i
              b. my parents and I
_____ 4. a. a famous movie director
              b. a director named steven spielberg
_____ 5. a. a clown named Rufus The Red
              b. a clown named Rufus the Red

EXERCISE 2   Correcting Errors in Capitalization

For each sentence below, correct all errors in capitalization. Write your corrections on the line below each sentence. Separate your answers with semicolons.

   EX.   In 2019, my parents and i went camping at big bend national park.
            I; Big Bend National Park
            _____

1. We left our home in norman, oklahoma, early in the Morning.

      _____

2. The air conditioner in our jeep stopped working as we crossed into texas.

      _____

3. My parents laughed when i rolled down the windows, and we drove all the way to the town of marathon that way.

      _____

4. After driving for over nine hours, we excitedly parked at panther junction, the Welcome Center for big bend national park.

      _____

5. Following the map, we made our way to a Campground next to the rio grande where we would stay for the week.

      _____

MODULE 13: CAPITAL LETTERS

PLACES AND PEOPLE

13c   **Capitalize geographical names.**

Type of Name	Examples
continents	North America, Asia
countries	Canada, Poland
cities, towns	Mexico City, Greenfield
states	Texas, North Dakota
islands	Oak Island, Maui
bodies of water	Sea of Japan, Persian Gulf
streets, highways	North Michigan Avenue, Skyline Drive
parks and forests	Turkey Swamp Park, Stokes State Forest
mountains	Rocky Mountains, Swiss Alps
sections of the country	the Midwest, the South

NOTE   In a hyphenated street number, the second part of the number is capitalized.

       EXAMPLE   East Twenty-Third Street

NOTE   Words such as *east, west, north,* or *south* are not capitalized when the words merely indicate directions.

       EXAMPLES   That street ends **south** of here. [direction]
                    These legends are told throughout the **West**. [section of the country]

13d   **Capitalize the names of planets, stars, and other heavenly bodies.**

EXAMPLES   Saturn, Betelgeuse, Milky Way

NOTE   Lowercase *sun* and *moon* and *earth*, except when *Earth* is used to name the planet.

       EXAMPLES   What on earth are you doing?
                    Mars is farther away from the Sun than Earth is.

13e   **Capitalize the names of persons.**

EXAMPLES   Sojourner Truth, Dolores Huerta, Ang Lee, Sacagawea

EXERCISE 3   Correcting Errors in Capitalization

For each sentence below, correct the errors in capitalization. Either change capital letters to lowercase letters or change lowercase letters to capital letters. Write your corrections on the line below each sentence. Separate your answers with a semicolon.

EX.   Someday I'd love to visit Arches National park in utah.
      <u>Arches National Park; Utah</u>

1. The country of tunisia is in the northern part of africa.

   _____

2. The city of boston sits by the atlantic ocean in the eastern part of massachusetts.

   _____

3. The novelist rosario ferré was born in puerto rico in 1938. she died there in 2016.

   _____

4. In science class, we watched a film by astonomer carl sagan about the beginnings of the solar system.

   _____

5. To get to times square, go north on fifth avenue to Forty-Second street.

   _____

6. Many famous writers in the united states were born in the south.

   _____

7. The island known as key west is located in the gulf of mexico.

   _____

8. The colorado river flows through grand canyon national park.

   _____

9. Not far to the West of washington, dc, are the blue ridge mountains.

   _____

10. Through a telescope, our teacher, Mr. Jiménez, showed us the planets saturn and jupiter.

   _____

GROUPS, ORGANIZATIONS, AND RELIGIONS

13f **Capitalize the names of organizations, teams, businesses, institutions, and government bodies.**

Type of Name	Examples
organizations	Academy of American Poets
teams	Minnesota Vikings
businesses	General Motors Corporation
institutions	Internal Revenue Service

NOTE   Do not capitalize words such as *hotel, theater,* and *middle school* unless they are part of the name of a particular building or institution.

EXAMPLES   Jefferson Middle School
your middle school

13g **Capitalize the names of nationalities, races, and peoples.**

EXAMPLES   French, Egyptian, Navajo, Hispanic

NOTE   The word *Black* may or may not be capitalized when it refers to people. Do not capitalize the word *white* when referring to people.

EXAMPLE   Jim Crow laws discriminated against Black [*or* black] people and benefited white people.

13h **Capitalize the names of religions and their followers, holy days, sacred writings, and specific deities.**

Type of Name	Examples
religions and followers	Islam, Christian, Hindu
holy days	Ramadan, Rosh Hashana
sacred writings	Koran, Upanishads, Bible
specific deities	God, Jehovah, Allah, Vishnu

NOTE   When referring to gods in general, or when using the word *god* descriptively, use lowercase.

EXAMPLE   The Roman god of war was named Mars.

EXERCISE 4   Proofreading Sentences for Correct Capitalization

For each sentence below, correct the errors in capitalization. Either change capital letters to lowercase letters or change lowercase letters to capital letters. Write your corrections on the line below each sentence. Separate your answers with a semicolon.

EX.   My brother went to the university of michigan for one year.

University of Michigan

1.   woodman middle school is the oldest school in the city.

_____

2.   The american automobile association will be closed Today.

_____

3.   Have you called the chamber of commerce about the parade?

_____

4.   Sara Donham is the minister at the congregational church.

_____

5.   When you visit Washington, DC, be sure to see the united states senate.

_____

EXERCISE 5   Identifying Correct Capitalization

For each of the pairs of phrases below, write the letter *C* on the line before each phrase that is capitalized correctly.

EX. _C_   a. Stay at the Shore Hotel.
    ____   b. Stay at the shore hotel.

____ 1. a. the Washington Spirit
____   b. the washington Spirit
____ 2. a. a jewish temple
____   b. a Jewish temple
____ 3. a. a Mexican dinner
____   b. a mexican dinner
____ 4. a. a large, nineteenth-century bible
____   b. a large, nineteenth-century Bible

MODULE 13: CAPITAL LETTERS
OBJECTS, EVENTS, STRUCTURES, AND AWARDS

13i   **Capitalize the brand names of business products.**

EXAMPLES   Healthy Choice soups, Canon copier [Notice that the names of the types of products are not capitalized.]

13j   **Capitalize the names of historical events and periods, special events, and calendar items.**

Type of Name	Examples
historical events and periods	Thirty Years' War, the Ice Age
special events and holidays	Cinco de Mayo, Election Day
calendar items	Flag Day

NOTE   Do not capitalize the name of a season unless it is part of a proper name.

        EXAMPLES   the spring rains
                       the Spring Writing Conference

13k   **Capitalize the names of ships, trains, airplanes, and spacecraft.**

Type of Name	Examples
ships	*Titanic, Seawise Giant*
trains	the General, Wabash Cannonball
airplanes	the Spirit of St. Louis, Concorde
spacecraft	Ranger 4, Orion

NOTE   In addition to being capitalized, the names of ships should be set in italics as shown above.

13l   **Capitalize the names of buildings and other structures.**

EXAMPLES   New York Public Library, Golden Gate Bridge

13m   **Capitalize the names of monuments and awards.**

Type of Name	Examples
Monuments	Vietnam Veterans Memorial
Awards	Academy Award

EXERCISE 6   Proofreading Sentences for Correct Capitalization

For each sentence below, correct the errors in capitalization. Either change capital letters to lowercase letters or change lowercase letters to capital letters. Write your corrections on the line below each sentence. Separate your answers with a semicolon.

EX.   My favorite holiday is cinco de mayo.
___Cinco de Mayo_____

1.   General Radwell awarded Carl the purple heart.
_____

2.   There will be fireworks and a picnic on the fourth of july.
_____

3.   The washington monument is over 555 feet high and is partly made of white marble.
_____

4.   For lunch, I had some swiss cheese and some carrot sticks.
_____

5.   My favorite Winter month is december.
_____

6.   Near the ice-skating rink was a sign announcing an upcoming event: the rockport winter carnival.
_____

7.   The white house is near the lincoln memorial.
_____

8.   The Fall leaves are quite beautiful, especially in the month of october.
_____

9.   One of Agatha Christie's novels took place on a train, the orient express.
_____

10. The poet Gwendolyn Brooks won the pulitzer prize in 1950.
_____

13n   Capitalize titles.

(1) Capitalize the title of a person when the title comes before the name.

EXAMPLES   **R**everend Martin Luther King Jr., **M**adame Curie

(2) Capitalize a word showing a family relationship only when the word is used before or in place of a person's name.

EXAMPLES   Ask if **U**ncle Horace will be there.
              I sent **M**om a nice card.

Do not capitalize a word showing a family relationship when a possessive such as *Bob's* or *your* comes before the word.

EXAMPLE   Can Bob's **s**ister and your **c**ousin Clara ride together?

(3) Capitalize the first and last words and all important words in titles of books, magazines, newspapers, poems, short stories, movies, television programs, works of art, and musical compositions.

Unimportant words in titles include:
  • articles (*a, an, the*)
  • coordinating conjunctions (*and, but, for, nor, or, so, yet*)
  • prepositions of fewer than five letters (such as *by, for, on, with*)

Type of Name	Examples
books	*Listen to the Crows*
magazines	*National Geographic*
newspapers	*the Baltimore Sun*
poems	"Another Mountain"
short stories	"The Gift of the Magi"
movies	*Finding Nemo*
television programs	*World News*
works of art	*Guernica*
musical compositions	"The Star-Spangled Banner"

NOTE   The article *the* before a title is not capitalized unless it is the first word of the title. For more about italics.

EXAMPLES   Here's the *Sumter County Journal*.
              Yes, I own **T**he **B**ook of Lists.

EXERCISE 7   Using Capital Letters in Titles

For each sentence below, correct the errors in capitalization. Either change capital letters to lowercase letters or change lowercase letters to capital letters. Write your corrections on the line below each sentence. Separate your answers with a semicolon.

EX. This latest issue of national geographic world is interesting.
National Geographic World _____

1. Yes, Professor, my sister donna was in your drawing class.

    _____

2. A review of that book, *the helen keller story,* appeared in a newspaper, *the beacon.*

    _____

3. My painting, called *the cattle driver,* is based on that old song "ghost riders in the sky."

    _____

4. Tomorrow grandfather Matsuda will speak on the topic "bridges in the garden."

    _____

5. My family reads *A christmas carol* and watches *Frosty The Snowman* around the holidays.

    _____

FIRST WORDS, PROPER ADJECTIVES, SCHOOL SUBJECTS

13o **Capitalize the first word in every sentence.**

EXAMPLES   **T**hose lilies look beautiful.
            My sister grew them.

The first word of a direct quotation should begin with a capital letter, whether or not the quotation starts the sentence.

EXAMPLE   Dezba announced, "**W**e found your key!"

13p **Capitalize proper adjectives.**

A *proper adjective* is formed from a proper noun and is always capitalized.

Proper Nouns	Proper Adjectives
China	Chinese art
Shakespeare	Shakespearean theater
Rome	Roman statues
Texas	Texas chili

13q **Do not capitalize the names of school subjects, except for official course names.**

EXAMPLES   art, science, Mathematics 101, Engineering I, German, Spanish

EXERCISE 8   Using Capital Letters Correctly

On the lines below, rewrite the following passage to correct all errors in the use of capital letters.

[1] In english we read a poem by an American poet. [2] The poem was about chinese porcelain. [3] according to the poet, pieces of beautiful, old porcelain sometimes wash up on the beach. [4] After we read this poem, i tried writing my own poem. [5] As my friend Marieka said, "it's interesting to think that these fragments came all the way across the ocean."

MODULE REVIEW

A. Correcting Errors in Capitalization

For each sentence below, correct the errors in capitalization. Either change capital letters to lowercase letters or change lowercase letters to capital letters. Write your corrections on the line below each sentence. Separate your answers with a semicolon.

EX. The name of our School football team is the mustangs.
school; Mustangs

1. The Doctor wrote an article that appeared in *contact* magazine.

2. Next year, i can take biology 1, which is taught by mrs. López.

3. This year, the bancroft science fair will be held at holder auditorium.

4. We asked Carl's Sister to bring in her model of an Ancient ship.

5. The film *A Night To Remember* was about the sinking of the *titanic*.

6. Did aunt Kate go to the same College in the midwest that your father went to?

7. Is the planet venus named after the roman goddess?

8. The Africa-America institute is on lexington avenue.

9. How many flags did the red, white, and blue company send us for our labor day parade?

10. Did nikki giovanni write the poem "Knoxville, tennessee"?

B. Proofreading a Paragraph for Correct Capitalization

In the following paragraph, all capital letters have been omitted. In the lines below, rewrite the paragraph, and add the necessary capital letters.

[1] last week the students at granville t. woods middle school celebrated international day. [2] one student, imani dobbey, sang nigerian folk songs. [3] another student sang songs from the appalachian mountains. [4] my cousin ruben brought in a poster showing the taj mahal, and mr. totsi showed us how to make sand paintings. [5] a reporter from the *daily word* visited our school and then wrote a story called "students celebrate the world."

_____

_____

_____

_____

_____

_____

_____

_____

_____

_____

_____

_____

_____

_____

_____

_____

MODULE 14: PUNCTUATION
END MARKS AND ABBREVIATIONS

An *end mark* is a mark of punctuation placed at the end of a sentence. *Periods, question marks, and exclamation points* are end marks.

14a   Use a period at the end of a statement.

EXAMPLE   A chef's salad usually contains meat, cheese, tomatoes, and greens.

14b   Use a question mark at the end of a question.

EXAMPLE   Did you call Kaloma yet?

14c   Use an exclamation point at the end of an exclamation.

EXAMPLE   What a wonderful dancer you are!

14d   Use either a period or an exclamation point at the end of a request or a command.

EXAMPLES   Please hold the door. [a request]
            Open the door this instant! [a command]

14e   Use periods after certain abbreviations.

Abbreviations with Periods	
Personal Names	E. B. White, Livie I. Durán
Titles Used with Names	Mrs., Ms., Mr., Dr., Jr., Sr.
Organizations and Companies	Co., Inc., Assoc.
Addresses	St., Rd., Ave., Bldg.
Times	a.m., Oct., Fri.
Abbreviations Without Periods	
Government Agencies	IRS, CIA, FBI
State Abbreviations	Seattle, WA 98009
Metric Units of Measure	kg, mm, cm
Certain Widely Used Abbreviations	NW, ATM, IQ, FM

NOTE   If you are not sure whether to use periods with abbreviations, look in a dictionary.

EXERCISE 1   Adding End Marks to Sentences

Write the end mark that should appear at the end of each sentence below.

EX.   Are you taking the bus or walking?

1. How brave those firefighters were
2. What authors do you like best
3. The art teacher will show us how to make dyes from natural ingredients
4. Hold this bandage against the wound and press firmly
5. Will Nayati enter the marathon again this year
6. Who was that on the telephone
7. The Fourth of July fireworks are fantastic
8. Tomorrow my mother is taking me to the game
9. When is the bus coming
10. Wow, what a great movie that was

EXERCISE 2   Proofreading for the Correct Use of Abbreviations

Add periods where needed in the items below. If the item needs no periods, write *C* on the line before it.

EX.   Dr. T. I. Livingstone

_____   1. Ms E A Rodríguez
_____   2. Parker Toy Co, Inc
_____   3. at 4:30 pm
_____   4. 5 ft 10 in tall
_____   5. turn NW after two blocks
_____   6. weighing 1 lb 4 oz
_____   7. at 13185 Mill Stone Dr
_____   8. outside the CIA building
_____   9. Lake Pleasant, NY 12108
_____ 10. Sam Dole, Sr

MODULE 14: PUNCTUATION

COMMAS IN A SERIES

End marks are used to separate complete thoughts. *Commas,* however, are used to separate words or groups of words (phrases and clauses) within a complete thought.

14f   Use commas to separate items in a series.

A series is a group of three or more items written one after another. The items in a series may be words, phrases, or clauses.

Words in a Series
Bread, cheese, and carrot sticks are in the basket.
The audience laughed, cried, and whistled.
Her trip was long, productive, and tiring.
Phrases in a Series
They learned to draw, to paint, and to sculpt.
People sat on tables, on chairs, and on the floor to hear him speak.
Dropped in cement, lost in high weeds, and run over by a truck, my lucky penny has seen some pretty hard times.
Clauses in a Series
I searched, I found, and I rejoiced.

14g   Use a comma to separate two or more adjectives that describe the same noun.

To see whether a comma is needed, insert *and* between the adjectives. If *and* sounds awkward, don't use a comma.

EXAMPLES   Your apartment is a cheerful, sunny place.

The letter was illustrated with small **stick figures**. [not *small, stick figures*]

EXERCISE 3   Proofreading Sentences for the Correct Use of Commas

Add or delete commas to correct the sentences below. If the sentence is correct, write *C* on the line before it.

EX. _____   Rafael's favorite activities are fishing, swimming, and watching TV.

_____ 1. Yori Bob and I enjoyed watching the rodeo last Saturday.

_____ 2. The actors wore large colorful masks made of wood.

_____ 3. My favorite vegetables include corn, tomatoes, and spinach.

_____ 4. Be sure to bring your bathing suit and a dry towel.

_____ 5. Several teachers volunteered to cook to serve and to clean up after the dinner.

_____ 6. The bus drove through Arkansas through Oklahoma and across Texas.

_____ 7. The trees bent over, the telephone poles cracked, and the fence blew away during the hurricane.

_____ 8. Someone extinguished the campfire covered it with sand and drenched it with water.

_____ 9. My father used to carry an old black lunch pail to school.

_____ 10. The Japanese gymnast was young strong and daring.

_____ 11. I want to learn to speak French, Spanish, and Chinese.

_____ 12. Hard work dedication and funding have made our project a success.

_____ 13. The costumes they wore were long colorful robes.

_____ 14. The clerk needs to know who you are where you live and when you moved here.

_____ 15. We need new erasers, and more chalk.

_____ 16. Have you been to her cool peaceful garden?

_____ 17. I found ants in the drawers, on the countertops, and under the cabinet.

_____ 18. The horse had a long, blond mane.

_____ 19. In this river, you can fish for bass trout or sunfish.

_____ 20. Where is a store that sells televisions surge protectors and adapters?

COMMAS WITH COMPOUND SENTENCES

14h   **Use a comma before *and, but, for, or, nor, so,* and *yet* when they join independent clauses in a compound sentence.**

EXAMPLE   Julius Lester rewrote the stories, and his publisher liked them.

When independent clauses are very short, the comma before *and, but,* or *or* may be omitted.

EXAMPLES   Chuck left but I stayed.
              The winds blew and the rain began.

NOTE   Do not use a comma if *for* is used as a preposition. Only use a comma before *for* when it is used as a conjunction combining two independent clauses (usually in formal situations).

              CONJUNCTION   The dove is a universal symbol, **for** it is associated with peace.
              PREPOSITION   We went to the store **for** more drinks.

Don't be confused by a simple sentence with a compound verb. A simple sentence has only one independent clause.

SIMPLE SENTENCE WITH   I **put** gas in the car and then **checked** the oil.
    COMPOUND VERB

COMPOUND SENTENCE   I put gas in the car, and then I checked the oil.
                           [two independent clauses]

EXERCISE 4   Correcting Compound Sentences by Adding Commas

For each of the following sentences add commas where they belong. If the sentence is correct, write *C* on the line before it.

   EX. _____   Vanilla is a great flavor, yet some people think it's boring.

_____ 1. The contest will not take place until June but we already have four entries.
_____ 2. Tree swallows can fly out of their nests and catch insects in midair.
_____ 3. They brought no meat or fish nor did they miss either one.
_____ 4. The bear sleeps during the winter and then comes out in the spring.
_____ 5. Our cabin was simple but it had three rooms.
_____ 6. People knew about the tomato yet they were afraid to eat it.
_____ 7. Our class learned drawing techniques before our teacher had us start painting.
_____ 8. The wind shifted, and it blew the rain in through our window.
_____ 9. Janell drew the pictures but another artist wrote the words.
_____ 10. We rested for an hour yet we were still tired.

EXERCISE 5   Combining Sentences

Rewrite each pair of sentences below as a single compound sentence. Use a comma and *and, but, or, so,* or *yet.*

EX.   The sun was hot. The breeze was cool.
    The sun was hot, but the breeze was cool.

1. I had plenty to eat. I still wanted fruit salad for desert.

    _____

2. My brother practices his violin every day. He is a wonderful musician.

    _____

3. I made dinner for my mother. My sister brought her flowers.

    _____

4. Janice plays soccer after school. She still does her homework.

    _____

5. You could walk in the park. You could walk on the beach.

    _____

6. It's supposed to rain today. The window is wide open.

    _____

7. My class will pick up trash from the schoolyard. We will return bottles for recycling.

    _____

8. Kieshia could enter her painting in the art show. She could enter her photographs.

    _____

9. The summer is going to be hot. I should go to the town pool often.

    _____

10. The restaurant was crowded Friday night. The service was still excellent.

    _____

COMMAS WITH SENTENCE INTERRUPTERS

14i **Use commas to set off an expression that interrupts a sentence.**

Two commas are needed if the expression to be set off comes in the middle of the sentence. One comma is needed if the expression comes first or last.

EXAMPLES   Thomas Hart Benton, the artist, lived there.

You know my cousin, of course.

14j **Use commas to set off nonessential participial phrases and nonessential subordinate clauses.**

A *nonessential* (or *nonrestrictive*) phrase or clause adds information that isn't needed to understand the meaning of the sentence.

NONESSENTIAL PHRASE   The messenger arrived late, **breathing rapidly.**

NONESSENTIAL CLAUSE   My necklace, **which you admired last week,** is made from fake gems and beads.

Do not set off *essential* (or *restrictive*) phrases or clauses. Since such a phrase or clause tells *which one(s)*, it cannot be omitted without changing the meaning of the sentence.

ESSENTIAL PHRASE   The dog **lurking near our garage** belongs to Tina. [*Which* dog?]

ESSENTIAL CLAUSE   Tyrone returned the ring **that I lost.** [*Which* ring?]

NOTE   A clause beginning with *that* is usually essential.

EXERCISE 6   Using Commas Correctly

The following sentences include an italicized phrase or clause. If the italicized phrase or clause is essential to the sentence, write *E* on the line before it. Write *NE* if the phrase or clause is nonessential. Insert commas where necessary.

EX.   __NE__   1. Washington, DC, *our nation's capital*, is an interesting city.

_____   1. The Empire State Building *which is featured in that movie* is in New York City.
_____   2. The book *that I liked best* is by Sandra Cisneros.
_____   3. The Monadnock Building *in Chicago* is a beautiful example of nineteenth-century public architecture.

_____ 4. Massachusetts *a small state in the Northeast* had the first public schools in the American colonies.

_____ 5. The plant *that is in my room* doesn't need much water.

_____ 6. Mark Juneau *who works on North Street* is a talented hair stylist.

_____ 7. The White Mountains *which are located in New Hampshire* are beautiful.

_____ 8. The bird *that you saw by the pond* was a snowy egret.

_____ 9. The bus driver *who drives Bus 48* found my folder.

_____ 10. Mt. Everest *which is located on the border of Tibet and Nepal* is the highest peak in the world.

_____ 11. The highway *that I talked about* is closed.

_____ 12. My aunt's car *which is ten years old* still runs well.

_____ 13. Edgar Allan Poe *who wrote many horror stories* died at an early age.

_____ 14. Is it the woman on my right *who is governor?*

_____ 15. The dress *that you sent* fits me.

_____ 16. This matter *which is very private* should not be discussed in public.

_____ 17. The athlete *who won the race* was Gwen Torrence.

_____ 18. Emma Willard *who founded one of the earliest women's schools for higher education in the United States* is an interesting subject for research.

_____ 19. The school's track *which needs repairs* was built in 1972.

_____ 20. Those *who lost their tickets* must wait outside.

OTHER USES OF THE COMMA

14k   Use commas to set off appositives and appositive phrases that are nonessential.

An *appositive* is a noun or a pronoun used to explain or identify another noun or pronoun.

EXAMPLES   Mel**, our nextdoor neighbor,** is also an old friend.
Parts of Windsor Castle, **one of the royal houses,** can be visited by tourists.

Do not use commas to set off an appositive that is essential to the meaning of a sentence.

ESSENTIAL   My brother **Lorenzo** finished the race first. [The speaker has more than one brother and must give a name to identify which brother.]

NONESSENTIAL   My brother, **Lorenzo,** finished the race first. [The speaker has only one brother and is giving his name as added information.]

EXERCISE 7   Proofreading Sentences for the Correct Use of Commas and Appositives

For each of the following sentences, underline the appositive phrase. Add commas where needed. [Hint: Not all of the appositives will require commas.]

EX.   The tree, <u>a sequoia</u>, is more than two hundred feet tall.

1. I asked Mr. Hatzidais my next-door neighbor about his hobby.
2. Did you know that Sophia my aunt used to have a beautiful tree in her yard?
3. The tree an American elm died of some disease.
4. Professor Smith-Rivera a biologist told me about the disease.
5. Did you know that Dutch elm disease a fungus can spread from tree to tree?

141   Use commas to set off words that are used in direct address.

EXAMPLES   **Akiva,** here is a test tube.

Let's see, **Elton,** where your seat is.

I know you can do it, **Riley.**

14m   Use commas to set off parenthetical expressions.

A *parenthetical expression* is a side remark that adds information or that relates ideas.

EXAMPLES   This water bottle, **I believe,** is Casey's.

For example, I donated six games to the toy drive.

EXERCISE 8   Correcting Sentences by Adding Commas

On the lines before each of the sentences below, write the parenthetical expressions. Include the needed commas.

EX. , by the way,   Penicillin by the way is a kind of mold.

_____   1. Today Louise we know the value of penicillin.

_____   2. By 1940 however this mold became a new medicine.

_____   3. Alexander Fleming I believe was the scientist who discovered the mold used in making penicillin.

_____   4. To tell the truth I don't know why he even noticed it.

_____   5. However the mold had ruined one of Fleming's experiments.

_____   6. You know many scientists might have thrown out an experiment like this.

_____   7. In fact the mold had killed the bacteria in part of the experiment.

_____   8. Nevertheless Fleming took a second look.

_____   9. This second look in my opinion showed a true growth mindset.

_____   10. On the other hand perhaps any hard-working scientist would have done the same.

MODULE 14: PUNCTUATION

MORE USES OF THE COMMA

14n   Use a comma after *yes, no,* or any mild exclamation, such as *well* or *why,* when it begins a sentence.

EXAMPLES   **Yes,** your answer is correct.

Why, you are just the person I was looking for.

14o   Use a comma after an introductory phrase.

EXAMPLES   **Starting next week,** Mario will be the monitor.

At the end of the story, there was a small note about the character.

14p   Use a comma after an introductory adverb clause.

An adverb clause that comes at the end of a sentence does not usually need a comma.

EXAMPLES   **Before you leave,** please feed the dog.

Please feed the dog **before you leave.**

14q   Use commas to separate items in dates and addresses.

A comma separates the last item in a date or an address from the words that follow it. However, a comma does not separate a month and a day (*December 5*), a state and its ZIP Code (*Utah 84767* or *UT 84767*), or a house number and its street name (*6385 Cedarwood Place*).

EXAMPLES   On **December 5, 2015,** we left for Canada.

I have lived at **6385 Cedarwood Place, Chico, California 95928,** for eight years.

EXERCISE 9   Adding Commas with Introductory Elements

Identify where commas belong in each sentence below. On the line before each sentence, write the word that is missing a comma after it and add the comma. Some sentences are correct as is. If the sentence is correct, write a *C* on the line.

EX. <u>store,</u>   In the store aisles were crammed with bargains.

_____   1. Shopping during the weekend I noticed many sales.
_____   2. Well most people pay more attention to nutrition now.
_____   3. In the chapter were many facts about food.
_____   4. When the weather is stormy our animals roam freely in the barn.
_____   5. At the end of one aisle I noticed a shelf of free pamphlets.
_____   6. The package from 101 Fifteenth Street Bradenton Florida 34206 must be from my uncle's store.
_____   7. During the week of January 3 2020 the owner gave free balloons to her customers.
_____   8. Because the bananas were soft Rory decided to make banana bread.
_____   9. You can bring your dog along if you want to.
_____ 10. Around this time of day I get very hungry.

EXERCISE 10   Using Commas Correctly

In the sentences below, insert commas wherever they are needed.

EX.   Nellie Ross was elected governor of Wyoming on November 4, 1924.

1. On May 24 1883 the Brooklyn Bridge opened.
2. You may write to me at 700 West State Street Burley ID 83318.
3. The Panama Canal first opened for shipping on August 15 1914 after years of hard work by many individuals.
4. We stopped in San Francisco California on our way to San Diego.
5. It wasn't until November 11 1918 that World War I finally ended.

REVIEW EXERCISE

A. Proofreading Sentences for the Correct Use of Commas

In the sentences below, insert commas where they are needed.

EX. We see, we hear, and we learn.

1. This book Marta is one that you should read.
2. It's about a doctor who worked in the country in several cities and on the battlefield.
3. Elizabeth Blackwell whom I admire was the doctor's name.
4. She must have been an intelligent determined woman.
5. She wanted to be a doctor but most schools would not train her.
6. Well it was hard for a woman to get a medical education then.
7. She went to medical school in Geneva New York in the 1840s.
8. She and Emily her sister both became doctors.
9. A doctor's life is varied challenging and rewarding.
10. If you would like to read about an interesting person choose a book about Elizabeth Blackwell a pioneering doctor.

B. Proofreading a Paragraph for Correct Use of Commas

In the following paragraph, insert commas where they are needed.

EX. Abi, have you ever heard of the Nazca Lines, which are in South America?

[1] The Nazca Lines huge drawings visible from the sky were made over 2000 years ago. [2] Known as geoglyphs these figures are carved into the surface of the earth. [3] The drawings cover nearly 200 square miles near the town of Nazca Peru. [4] The images include a hummingbird a monkey a whale trees flowers and geometric shapes. [5] Because the people who made them could not have viewed them from the air many people have speculated about their purpose. [6] Some people believe it or not even thought they might be evidence of extraterrestrials! [7] What could they be for I wonder? [8] Walking the paths of the drawings people say is an amazing experience. [9] The dry climate in their location southern Peru has preserved the drawings for centuries. [10] UNESCO part of the United Nations recognized the significance of the Nazca Lines by declaring it a World Heritage site.

C. Writing Notes for an Article

The new Time Travel Amusement Park is opening in your city. Your local newspaper wants you to write a feature article about the opening day. As you walk through the park, you listen to people talking. Imagine and write down their comments and impressions about exhibits, as well as your own thoughts.

1. Think about what exhibits might fill the Time Travel Amusement Park. Research or invent locations and dates of the exhibits.
2. Create at least five sentences about the park. You might want to include things that you overhear and your thoughts about what you see. Include sentences with introductory words and phrases, interrupters, appositives, direct address, or parenthetical expressions.
3. Be sure that your sentences include all necessary commas.

EX.   For opening day, crowds of people lined up inside the park gate.
       Look, there's a spacecraft and a skywalk!

_____

_____

_____

_____

_____

_____

_____

_____

_____

_____

_____

_____

_____

_____

_____

_____

A *semicolon* looks like a combination of a period and a comma, and that is just what it is. A semicolon separates complete thoughts as a period does. A semicolon also separates items within a sentence as a comma does.

14r   Use a semicolon to join two independent clauses.

EXAMPLES   Maya looked outside and sighed; rain was still falling.
The train pulled into the station; only one person got out.

14s   Use a semicolon before a coordinating conjunction to join independent clauses that contain commas.

CONFUSING   I brought lettuce, tomatoes, and carrots, but bread, milk, and cheese were donated.

CLEAR   I brought lettuce, tomatoes, and carrots; but bread, milk, and cheese were donated.

NOTE   Semicolons are most effective when they are not overused. Sometimes it is better to separate a compound sentence or a heavily punctuated sentence into two sentences rather than use a semicolon.

ACCEPTABLE   The wind blows the sand around and causes the grains to rub against each other; the constant rubbing gradually shapes each grain, making it rounder as time goes on.

BETTER   The wind blows the sand around and causes the grains to rub against each other. The constant rubbing gradually shapes each grain, making it rounder as time goes on.

EXERCISE 11   Using Semicolons Correctly

On the lines before each of the sentences below, write the words before and after the missing semicolon. Insert a semicolon between these words.

EX.   _yet; I'm_   I haven't posted my dance video yet I'm nervous about sharing it.

_____   1. Let's have the picnic in the evening it's too hot earlier.

_____   2. I spent all weekend finishing the project that's why I didn't text you back.

_____   3. My dog is so funny she barks when she's dreaming.

_____   4. The fall play will be a musical I'm practicing a song for my audition.

_____   5. Our reading assignment is a choice novel we can pick a book from a long list of options.

_____   6. I can't hang out this weekend my aunt is visiting from Mexico.

_____   7. Lots of people were late to school today because they missed their alarms the power went out last night.

_____   8. My favorite white t-shirt is now pink it accidentally got washed with my red soccer socks.

_____   9. The birds in this area are varied for example we see parakeets, hummingbirds, cardinals, and painted buntings.

_____ 10. That's a great climbing tree it has lots of low horizontal branches.

COLONS

14t **Use a colon before a list of items, especially after expressions such as *the following* or *as follows*.**

EXAMPLES   Please bring these items to the day camp: a towel, a hat, a swimsuit, and a water bottle.

We will provide the following: healthy snacks, a lunch, sunscreen, and craft supplies.

Never use a colon directly after a verb or a preposition. Omit the colon, or reword the sentence.

INCORRECT   In the next exhibit, look at: the pond, the shore, the high grass, and the sand.

CORRECT   In the next exhibit, look at these areas: the pond, the shore, the high grass, and the sand.

14u **Use a colon between the hour and the minute.**

EXAMPLE   It is now 3:30 p.m.   We will leave at 6:00 a.m.

14v **Use a colon after the salutation of a business letter.**

EXAMPLE   Dear Dr. Gaetano: Dear Reference Librarian:

EXERCISE 12   Using Colons and Commas Correctly

On the line below each of the following incomplete sentences, write a complete sentence by adding the information suggested in brackets. Insert colons and commas where they are needed. [Hint: before a list of items, you might need to add words such as *the following*.]

EX.   My favorite show begins at [*time*].
My favorite show begins at 8:00 p.m.

1. We have visited these stores [*list*].

   _____

2. I go to bed at [*time*].

   _____

3. "[*salutation*]" is the greeting line of this business letter.

   _____

4. I am going to the park to exercise with Dakota, and I'll be home at [*time*].

   _____

5. Jennifer gave invitations to these people [*list*].

_____

6. In English class this year, we are going to read these books [*list*].

_____

7. The basketball game starts at [*time*].

_____

8. This summer vacation, I am going to do these things [*list*].

_____

9. I try to exercise every day at [*time*].

_____

10. The activities that I enjoy are the following [*list*].

_____

MODULE 14: PUNCTUATION
MODULE REVIEW

A.   Proofreading Sentences for the Correct Use of Commas

For each of the sentences below, add commas where needed.

> EX.   Well, I just heard a strange story.

1. Look at all the ostriches Raoul.
2. There are ostrich farms in Arizona Arkansas California and Texas.
3. These birds are large powerful animals.
4. On September 12 1882 a New York newspaper wrote a story about ostrich feathers.
5. Anaheim California was the location of the first ostrich farm in the United States.
6. The first baby ostrich which belonged to Billie Frantz was born on July 4 1883.
7. By the end of 1911 there were more than six thousand ostriches in the United States.
8. Feathers which are clipped not plucked are harvested every eight or nine months.
9. Ostrich feathers which are used as decoration are in demand.
10. They decorate hats fans feather dusters and several other items.

B.   Using End Marks, Commas, Semicolons, and Colons Correctly in a Paragraph

The sentences in the following paragraph need end marks, commas, semicolons, or colons. Add the missing punctuation.

Tucked away in the backyard of an ordinary house in an ordinary Austin Texas neighborhood is something extraordinary Known as the Cathedral of Junk the enormous work of art has grown and changed over three decades The many-roomed tower is built entirely from junk for example it includes dolls crutches musical instruments and pieces of decorative railings It's surprising to think that something so big and elaborate is the work of only one person Over the years its builder Vince Hannemann has faced many obstacles complaints from neighbors concerns about safety and his lack of free time to build The structure is stronger than people might expect however Would you believe it can withstand hurricane-force winds It's amazing I think that places like this exist

C. Proofreading a Letter

Some parts of the letter below need end marks, commas, semicolons, or colons. Add the missing punctuation marks.

710 Lakeport Drive
Stony Point, NY 10980
August 22, 2023

Dr. Emil Valdez
3486 Wichita Place
Haverstraw, NY 10927

Dear Dr. Valdez:

  My school, Fieldstone Middle School, has a science fair every year. This year it will be held on October 10, 2023, in the school auditorium. Fair entries include the following four categories: the heavens, our planet, water, and machines. What a wonderful crowd we had last year! This year, however, we'd like to make the fair even better. This desire to improve our fair is why I am writing to you, Dr. Valdez.

  Last month my uncle Lokela heard you speak about diets and young people. He thought you were an excellent speaker, and he found the topic fascinating. Well, my class wants you for its speaker. Would you give the speech at our science fair? We would schedule a time between 1:30 and 3:30 p.m. We could pick you up at the airport, drive you to the fair, and take you back to the airport. We would also include your name on our list of sponsors. I hope you will accept our offer. Please let us know before September 8, 2023.

Sincerely,
Irma Lukas

ITALICS

Italics are printed letters that lean to the right—*like this*. If your work is handwritten, you show that a word should be *italicized* by <u>underlining</u> it.

15a **Use italics for titles of books, plays, periodicals, films, television programs, works of art, long musical compositions, and ships.**

Type of Name	Examples
Books	*The Hobbit, Dear Martin*
Plays	*The Hitchhiker, Lost in Yonkers*
Periodicals	*Newsweek,* the *Atlanta Journal-Constitution*
Films	*Dream Horse, Hidden Figures*
Television Programs	*Ms. Marvel, Stranger Things*
Works of Art	*Infinity Mirrors, Forever Bicycles*
Long Musical Compositions	*Renaissance, Appalachian Spring*
Ships	the *Lusitania,* the USS *Constitution*

NOTE   Names of aircraft, trains, and spacecraft are capitalized but not italicized.

        EXAMPLE   Air Force One, Acela Express

NOTE   The article *the* is often written before a title but is not capitalized unless it is part of the official title.

        EXAMPLE   I agreed with the editorial in *The Denver Post.*

15b **Use italics for words, letters, and figures referred to as such.**

EXAMPLES   The word ***mask*** has several meanings.

                Do you know a word that contains the vowels ***a, e, i, o,*** and ***u***?

                Write an ***8*** in the last column.

EXERCISE 1   Using Italics (Underlining) Correctly

For each sentence below, underline each word or item that should be italicized.

    EX.   Willy has the lead role in <u>Fiddler on the Roof</u>.

1. I read the last module of Barrio Boy for homework.
2. A popular television show in the 1950s was I Love Lucy.
3. Yesterday, the San Francisco Examiner had an informative article about electric vehicles.
4. Annie misspelled the word license in her report.
5. Winslow Homer's painting Snap the Whip is displayed at the Metropolitan Museum of Art.

6. In English class, we watched the film To Kill a Mockingbird.
7. Mozart composed the score for the opera The Marriage of Figaro.
8. Is there one p in the name Mississippi?
9. The play Raisin in the Sun was written by Lorraine Hansberry.
10. In 2021, the ship Ever Given ran aground and blocked the Suez Canal for nearly a week.

EXERCISE 2   Proofreading a Paragraph for the Correct Use of Italics

In the paragraph below, underline each word or item that should be italicized.

EX.   We went to the space museum and saw an exhibition about <u>New Horizons</u>.

[1] Darryl and I looked through The Boston Globe and The Salem News. [2] This weekend we could see the play Our Town or the ballet version of Romeo and Juliet. [3] I had read a book called The Art of Thornton Wilder about Our Town's writer. [4] Of course, we could stay home and watch an episode of Nature that is on television tonight. [5] We finally decided to take a ride on a ship called the Spirit of Boston.

MODULE 15: PUNCTUATION

QUOTATION MARKS

15c   **Use quotation marks to enclose a direct quotation—a person's exact words.**

Be sure to place quotation marks both before and after a person's exact words.

EXAMPLES   In *Poor Richard's Almanack*, Ben Franklin advised his readers, "Early to bed and early to rise, makes a man healthy, wealthy, and wise."

                "Do you know what you would do," asked the guide, "if you came face to face with a big bear?"

15d   **A direct quotation begins with a capital letter.**

EXAMPLES   Emilio said, "**A** place I'd like to visit is the Volcán Santiago National Park in Nicaragua."

                In a book about the early history of the Americas, the author states, "**P**eople made clay popcorn poppers two thousand years ago."

15e   **When a quoted sentence is interrupted by the expression identifying the speaker, the continuation of the sentence begins with a lowercase letter.**

EXAMPLES   "The village," explained Kali, "**i**s surrounded by rice fields and farmland."

                "When you leave the house," added Chris, "**l**ock the door."

A quoted sentence that is divided in this way is called a *broken quotation*. Notice that each part of a broken quotation is enclosed in a set of quotation marks. When the second part of a divided quotation is a sentence, it begins with a capital letter.

EXAMPLE   "Sit down," directed Taylor. "**T**he concert is about to begin."

15f   **A direct quotation is set off from the rest of the sentence by a comma, a question mark, or an exclamation point. Only use a period if the quotation ends the sentence.**

EXAMPLES   Shane said**,** "We're studying rain forests."

                "Everyone should learn about them**,**" suggested Alexis.

                "Why are they so important**?**" asked Jalene.

                "Rain forests teem with life**!**" exclaimed Vincent.

15g   **A period or a comma should always be placed inside the closing quotation marks.**

EXAMPLES   Mateo replied, "My appointment is next week."

                      "I'm going for my yearly checkup today," said Gina.

15h   **A question mark or an exclamation point should be placed inside the closing quotation marks when the quotation itself is a question or an exclamation. Otherwise, it should be placed outside.**

EXAMPLES   "Where is the trail?" asked the hiker. [The quotation is a question.]

                      Who said, "Drafts cause colds"? [The sentence, not the quotation, is a question.]

When both the sentence and a quotation at the end of the sentence are questions (or exclamations), only one question mark (or exclamation point) is used. It is placed inside the closing quotation marks.

EXAMPLE   Did Kayla ask, "How do I get to Central Park from here?"

EXERCISE 3   Punctuating Quotations

For each sentence below, insert quotation marks and other marks of punctuation where needed.

EX.   **"This year," said Chen, "is going to be the Year of the Dragon."**

1. Lim Sing is looking forward to the Festival of Lanterns said her father
2. Chen replied I received calendars from relatives in Hong Kong
3. If you look closely at them he explained you can see each day's lunar date written in Chinese.
4. Will you help me cook the special roasted seeds and dried fruits Mother bought for the New Year's meal asked Lim Sing
5. Wow exclaimed Chen This celebration is my favorite time of the year

15i   **When you write dialogue (conversation), begin a new paragraph every time the speaker changes.**

EXAMPLE   The clerk smiled up at Luis. "Can I help you?"

"I'm here to file my paperwork to run for office," he nervously replied.

"Let's see what you have," she said, reaching for the papers. "It looks like everything is in order."

Luis breathed a sigh of relief and said, "I've never done this before."

"Well, you've done the first step," the clerk reassured him. "Good luck!"

15j   **When a quotation consists of several sentences, put quotation marks only at the beginning and the end of the whole quotation.**

EXAMPLE   "The fundamentals are what matter the most! Are your free throws going into the basket 100% of the time? If not, you need more practice," urged Coach Hobbs.

15k   **Use single quotation marks to enclose a quotation within a quotation.**

EXAMPLE   Seth explained, "The photographer said, 'You must observe the world around you very closely.'"

15l   **Use quotation marks to enclose the titles of short works such as short stories, poems, articles, songs, and episodes that are part of a television, radio, or podcast series.**

EXAMPLES   Countee Cullen's poem "Incident" describes a child's experience of racism.
Will you sing "America the Beautiful" at the assembly?

EXERCISE 4   Punctuating Quotations

Insert quotation marks where needed in each of the following sentences.

EX.   "Read the module 'Edge of the Sea' for homework," said Mrs. Zayas.

1. Last night I read the story The Last Leaf to my sister, said Nora.

2. Marian Anderson once sang America at the Lincoln Memorial.

3. Who said, An apple a day keeps the doctor away? asked Meli.

4. Mr. Ryder said, The last module in *Anne of Avonlea* is A Wedding at the Stone House.

5. Sarah said, This will be a busy weekend. We are planting beach grass on the dunes to hold the sand in place. The grass will also help the dunes grow higher.

EXERCISE 5   Punctuating Paragraphs

Rewrite the paragraph below, using quotation marks and other marks of punctuation wherever necessary. Remember to begin a new paragraph each time the speaker changes. [Note: The punctuation marks that are already included in the exercise are correct.]

EX.   I wish I didn't have a summer birthday! exclaimed Ayesha.
      "I wish I didn't have a summer birthday!" exclaimed Ayesha.

[1] It's so hard to plan a party when everyone is on summer break, lamented Ayesha. [2] And it's always so hot, too. [3] Well, interjected her friend Erin, at least you don't have to go to school on your birthday! [4] True, replied Ayesha thoughtfully. [5] That's definitely nice. [6] And, Erin added, your birthday is a great excuse to get together over the break, even if it isn't for a big party. [7] Ayesha suddenly smiled. [8] You're right, she exclaimed. [9] I can have a bunch of small get-togethers instead of one big party. [10] Yes, Erin laughed, you can make it a birth-month celebration!

_____

_____

_____

_____

_____

_____

_____

_____

_____

_____

_____

_____

_____

_____

_____

_____

APOSTROPHE

The *possessive case* of a noun or a pronoun shows ownership or relationship.

Ownership	Relationship
Lenny's desk	a **week's** pay
the **player's** score	**our** parents
her sweater	**cat's** paw
everyone's test	two **cents'** worth

15m To form the possessive case of a singular noun, add an apostrophe and an *s*.

EXAMPLES   the man**'s** shirt   Georgia**'s** painting
                   a friend**'s** house   Gary**'s** idea

NOTE   Add *'s* to singular nouns that are possessive, even if a proper noun ends in *s*.

                   EXAMPLES   Kansas's parks   Frances's birthday   the bus's wheels

15n To form the possessive case of a plural noun ending in *s*, add only the apostrophe.

EXAMPLES   friends' names   two years' practice   two enemies' plans
                   wolves' tracks   the Ryans' cottage   artists' paintings

15o To form the possessive case of a plural noun that does not end in *s*, add an apostrophe and an *s*.

EXAMPLES   women**'s** suits   people**'s** faces   children**'s** books
                   deer**'s** tails   geese**'s** wings   moose**'s** antlers

NOTE   Do not use an apostrophe to form the plural of a noun. Remember that the apostrophe shows ownership or relationship.

                   INCORRECT   Two girls' have red coats.

                   CORRECT   Two **girls** have red coats.

                   CORRECT   The two **girls'** coats are red.

15p Do not use an apostrophe with possessive personal pronouns.

EXAMPLES   Is that dog **theirs**?
                   Is the pen **his** or **hers**?

EXERCISE 6   Using Apostrophes for Singular Possessives

In each sentence in the paragraph below, underline the word that needs an apostrophe, and insert the apostrophe.

EX.   The Spanish galleon was one of the <u>world's</u> greatest ships.

[1] A sailors life on a galleon was hard and uncomfortable. [2] The captains orders had to be obeyed without question. [3] On a voyage, a mariners strength and courage were put to the test. [4] A single days work left all on board exhausted. [5] Sailors raised the galleons sails by pulling on heavy ropes. [6] If the wind picked up, the sails had to be lowered without a moments delay. [7] While the ship rolled violently, sailors climbed the masts rigging. [8] In rough seas, the ships timbers moved. [9] Often, the hulls seams opened, letting in a flood of water. [10] Because the crews sleeping quarters were below the waterline, sailors often had to sleep in wet, smelly bunks.

EXERCISE 7   Writing Possessives

Rewrite each of the expressions below by using the possessive case. Be sure to insert apostrophes in the right places.

EX.   the records of the singer   <u>   the singer's records   </u>

1. the tools of the carpenters   _____
2. the tails of the mice   _____
3. the towel that belongs to Fatima _____
4. the office of the coach   _____
5. the toys of the children   _____

MODULE 15: PUNCTUATION

OTHER USES OF THE APOSTROPHE

A *contraction* is a shortened form of a word, a number, or a group of words.

15q **Use an apostrophe to show where letters, numbers, or words have been omitted (left out) in a contraction.**

Common Contractions	
I am.....................................I'm	where is ....where's
let us ....let's	we are ....we're
she would......................she'd	he is ....he's
they had ....they'd	you will ....you'll

The word *not* can be shortened to *n't* and added to a verb, usually without any change in the spelling of the verb.

EXAMPLES   is not................... is**n't**   has not......................has**n't**
does not...........does**n't**   would not ....would**n't**

EXCEPTIONS will not..............wo**n't**   cannot........................can**'t**

Be careful not to confuse contractions with possessive pronouns.

Contractions	Possessive Pronouns
It's your book.	**Its** tail is long and bushy.
You're early.	**Your** dinner is ready.
They're here.	**Their** name is Yahada.
There's Mom.	That book is **theirs**.

15r **Use an apostrophe and an *s* to form the plurals of letters.**

EXAMPLES   I sometimes write *g***'s** for *q***'s**.

This semester Evey earned all A**'s** and B**'s**.

15s **Use only an *s* to form the plurals of numbers or abbreviations.**

EXAMPLES   I love listening to music from the 1980**s**.

Her dives were nearly perfect—she scored mostly 9**s**.

EXERCISE 8   Using Apostrophes in Contractions Correctly

For each of the sentences below, underline the word or words requiring an apostrophe, and insert the apostrophe. If the sentence is correct, write *C* on the line before the sentence.

EX. _____   You <u>can't</u> believe everything you read or hear.

_____ 1. Should you drink water while youre exercising?
_____ 2. Some people think they shouldnt drink any liquids.
_____ 3. They think water will bloat them, and they won't be able to run fast.
_____ 4. You musnt pay any attention to these people because theyre mistaken.
_____ 5. Now well find out why.
_____ 6. When you're running or exercising hard, your body loses fluids very quickly.
_____ 7. Youll get sick or even faint if you get dehydrated.
_____ 8. Lets use some common sense.
_____ 9. Dont forget to replace the missing fluids.
_____ 10. The next time youre playing hard, drink some water.

EXERCISE 9   Writing Contractions

On the line before each sentence, write a contraction for each italicized word or word pair.

EX. <u>we're</u>   In biology class, *we are* studying life in the oceans.

_____ 1. Sunlight *cannot* reach the depths of the ocean.
_____ 2. Because *there is* no light near the ocean floor, many animals that live in the deep ocean create their own light, like fireflies.
_____ 3. *What is* the strangest creature in the deep ocean?
_____ 4. *I am* convinced that the oddest of them all is the angler fish.
_____ 5. *It is* able to attract prey using a dorsal fin that dangles above its mouth.

MODULE REVIEW

A. Proofreading for the Correct Use of Apostrophes, Quotation Marks, and Underlining (Italics)

Rewrite each of the following sentences so that apostrophes, quotation marks, and underlining are used correctly. [Note: A sentence may contain more than one error.]

EX.   Dont mix up the words symbol and cymbal, said Jesse.
       "Don't mix up the words <u>symbol</u> and <u>cymbal</u>," said Jesse.

1. When I watched my baby cousin, I read to her from my favorite old book, Frog and Toad Are Friends.

2. Amals skateboard may be old, but she uses it for some amazing tricks.

3. Did Mr. Vela say Read Chapter 5 asked Marika.

4. I always want to pronounce the *ss* at the ends of Arkansas and Des Moines.

5. Are you sure, Mom asked, that this jacket is yours?

6. My friend Dray used free software to make an album he titled Drays Gaze.

7. Dad is reading an article titled How Everything Has Changed from todays Miami Herald.

   _____

   _____

8. Mosess backpack was left under his desk during the fire drill. _____

   _____

   _____

9. When they came back inside, both cats paws were muddy. _____

   _____

   _____

10. Do you agree with the old saying, Beauty is in the eye of the beholder? _____

    _____

    _____

MODULE 16: SPELLING
THE DICTIONARY

A dictionary entry is divided into several parts. Study the parts of the following sample dictionary entry:

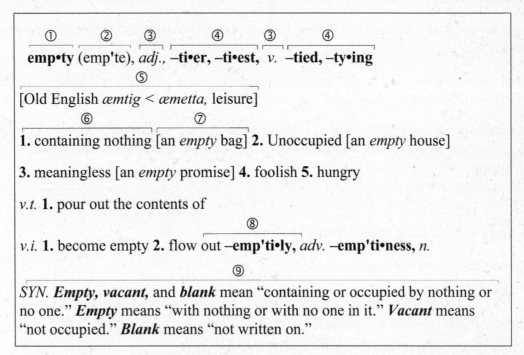

1. **Entry word.** The entry word shows the correct spelling of the word. An alternate spelling may also be shown. The entry word shows how the word should be divided into syllables and may also show if the word should be capitalized.

2. **Pronunciation.** The pronunciation is shown using accent marks, phonetic symbols, or diacritical marks. Each *phonetic symbol* represents a specific sound. *Diacritical marks* are special symbols placed above letters to show how those letters sound. Every dictionary provides a guide to the symbols and marks it uses. Many online dictionaries feature audio to hear the correct pronunciation of the word.

3. **Part-of-speech labels.** Some words may be used as more than one part of speech. In this case, a part-of-speech label is also given before the set of definitions that matches each label. In the sample entry, *empty* can be used as an adjective or a verb, depending on the meaning.

4. **Other forms.** Sometimes a dictionary shows spellings of plural forms of nouns, tenses of verbs, or the comparative forms of adjectives and adverbs.

5. **Etymology.** The *etymology* tells about the historical development of a word, by determining its basic elements. In the sample entry, *empty* comes from the Old English. The etymology also shows how the word has changed over time.

6. **Definitions.** If there is more than one meaning, definitions are numbered or lettered.

7. **Sample usage.** Some dictionaries include sample phrases to illustrate particular meanings of words.

8. **Related word forms.** These are forms of the entry word created by adding suffixes or prefixes. Sometimes dictionaries also list common phrases in which the word appears.

9. **Synonyms and antonyms.** Words similar in meaning are *synonyms.* Words opposite in meaning are *antonyms.* Many dictionaries list synonyms and antonyms at the end of some word entries.

EXERCISE 1   Using a Dictionary

Use a dictionary to answer the questions below.

EX.   How many syllables are in the word *indignation*? _____four_____

1. How is the word *serious* divided into syllables? _____
2. What is the spelling for the plural form of *armadillo*? _____
3. What are three different meanings for the word *peck*? _____

   _____

4. What is the past tense of *awake*? _____
5. When should the word *cupid* be capitalized? _____

EXERCISE 2   Writing Words with Alternate Spellings

Write the alternate spelling for each of the words below on the line after the word. Use a dictionary as needed.

EX.   pickax   <u>pickaxe</u>

1. enroll   _____
2. catalog   _____
3. hurrah   _____
4. whiz   _____
5. judgment   _____

SPELLING RULES

ie and ei

16a   Write *ie* when the sound is long *e*, except after *c*.

EXAMPLES   field, belief, grief, thief, receipt, ceiling
EXCEPTIONS   neither, either, seize, leisure, weird

16b   Write *ei* when the sound is not long *e*, especially when the sound is long *a*.

EXAMPLES   neighbor, vein, eight, reign, height, foreign
EXCEPTIONS   pie, tie, friend, mischief

-cede, -ceed, and -sede

16c   The only word ending in *-sede* is *supersede*. The only words ending in *-ceed* are *exceed*, *proceed*, and *succeed*. All other words with this sound end in *-cede*.

EXAMPLES   recede, concede, intercede, precede

EXERCISE 3   Writing Words with *ie* and *ei*

On the line in each word, write the letters *ie* or *ei* to spell each word correctly. Use a dictionary as needed.

EX. br <u>ie</u> f

1. sh _____ ld
2. fr _____ ght
3. p _____ r
4. sl _____ gh

5. y _____ ld
6. p _____ ce
7. rev _____ w
8. w _____ ght

9. rec _____ ve
10. fr _____ nd

EXERCISE 4   Proofreading a Paragraph to Correct Spelling Errors

The paragraph below contains ten spelling errors. Underline the misspelled words. Write the correct spelling above each misspelled word. Use a dictionary as needed.

                                   neighborhood
EX. Everyone in Pepita's <u>nieghborhood</u> was looking forward to *Carnival*.

[1] The sight on the street exceded the vision she remembered, and Pepita could hardly believe her eyes. [2] For a breif moment, she thought she was back in Trinidad. [3] The street was crowded with people dressed in thier colorful masks and costumes. [4] They liesurely strolled around, waiting for the parade to begin. [5] Pepita beleived that she recognized the steel band on a platform halfway down the street. [6] She knew several of the musicians, who were from iether Trinidad or Barbados. [7] Sheilding her eyes from the late-afternoon sun, Pepita paused and listened to the calypso beat. [8] She had to conceed that the band sounded as good as any group back home on the island. [9] Suddenly, a freind seized her hand. [10] "Here," said Marita, "try a peice of this fish."

MODULE 16: SPELLING

PREFIXES AND SUFFIXES

A *prefix* is a letter or a group of letters added to the beginning of a word to change its meaning. A *suffix* is a letter or a group of letters added to the end of a word to change its meaning.

16d   **When adding a prefix to a word, do not change the spelling of the word itself.**

EXAMPLES   mis + place = **mis**place   dis + satisfy = **dis**satisfy
                 un + happy = **un**happy   im+ mortal = **im**mortal

16e   **When adding the suffix *-ness* or *-ly* to a word, do not change the spelling of the word itself.**

EXAMPLES   thick + ness = thick**ness**   dry + ness = dry**ness**
                 week + ly = week**ly**   soft + ly = soft**ly**

EXCEPTION   For most words that end in *y*, change the *y* to *i* before *-ly* or *-ness*.
            EXAMPLES   sloppy + ness = slopp**iness**   easy + ly = eas**ily**

16f   **Drop the final silent *e* before a suffix beginning with a vowel.**

Vowels are the letters *a, e, i, o, u,* and sometimes *y*. All other letters of the alphabet are *consonants*.

EXAMPLES   large + est = larg**est**   write + ing = writ**ing**
                 like + able = lik**able**   slice + er = slic**er**

EXCEPTION   Keep the silent *e* in words ending in *ce* and *ge* before a suffix beginning with *a* or *o*.

            EXAMPLES   service + able = servic**eable**
                        outrage + ous = outrag**eous**

16g   **Keep the final *e* before a suffix beginning with a consonant.**

EXAMPLES   use + less = use**less**   nine + ty = nin**ety**
                 peace + ful = peac**eful**   safe + ly = saf**ely**

EXCEPTIONS   argue + ment = argu**ment**   true + ly = tru**ly**

EXERCISE 5   Spelling Words with Prefixes and Suffixes

On the line after each partial word equation, write the word with the given prefix or suffix that creates a new word.

EX.   cheerful + ly   <u>cheerfully</u>

1. new + ness _____
2. real + ly _____
3. un + clear _____
4. over + spend _____
5. final + ly _____
6. loud + ness _____
7. over + ripe _____
8. playful + ness _____
9. friendly + ness _____
10. ir + regular _____

11. mis + spell _____
12. im + perfect _____
13. heavy + ness _____
14. dis + able _____
15. in + formal _____
16. joyful + ly _____
17. steady + ly _____
18. in + complete _____
19. last + ly _____
20. shy + ness _____

EXERCISE 6   Spelling Words with Suffixes

On the line after each partial word equation, write the word with the given suffix that creates a new word.

EX.   plenty + ful   <u>plentiful</u>

1. noisy + ly _____
2. believe + ing _____
3. hope + ful _____
4. strange + est _____
5. graze + ing _____
6. pave + ment _____
7. polite + ness _____
8. waste + ful _____
9. adore + able _____
10. busy + ly _____

11. amaze + ing _____
12. hasty + ly _____
13. measure + ment _____
14. courage + ous _____
15. drive + er _____
16. angry + ly _____
17. brave + er _____
18. little + est _____
19. change + able _____
20. care + ful _____

MODULE 16: SPELLING
SUFFIXES

16h   **For words ending in *y* preceded by a consonant, change the *y* to *i* before any suffix that does not begin with *i*.**

EXAMPLES   merry + ment = merr**iment**   worry + ing = worry**ing**
                      hasty + ly = hast**ily**

Words ending in *y* preceded by a vowel do not change their spelling before a suffix.

  EXAMPLES   obey + ed = obe**yed**   play + ful = pla**yful**
EXCEPTIONS   pay + ed = pa**id**   day + ly = da**ily**

16i   **Double the final consonant before adding *-ing*, *-ed*, *-er*, or *-est* to a one-syllable word that ends in a single consonant preceded by a single vowel.**

EXAMPLES   hot + est = ho**tt**est   sad + er = sa**dd**er
                      drip + ed = dri**pp**ed   hop + ed + ho**pp**ed

In a word with one syllable, double the final consonant only if the word ends in one vowel and one consonant.

EXAMPLES   hard + er = har**d**er   quick + est = quick**est**
                      bump + ing = bum**p**ing   start + ed = start**ed**

EXERCISE 7   Spelling Words with Suffixes

On the line after each partial word equation, write each word, with the given suffix that makes a new word.

   EX.   swim + er   <u>swimmer</u>

1. dizzy + ness _____
2. grin + ing _____
3. skid + ed _____
4. fresh + er _____
5. rusty + est_____

6. key + ed _____
7. multiply + ing _____
8. cheer + ed _____
9. lazy + er_____
10. stay + ed _____

EXERCISE 8   Identifying Incorrect Spelling in a Paragraph

The paragraph below contains ten spelling errors. Underline the incorrect words. Then write the correct spelling above the incorrect word. Use a dictionary as needed.

hottest
EX.   I think Saturday must have been the <u>hotest</u> day of the year so far.

[1] The temperature was ninety-five and still riseing. [2] My fruit juice icy popsicle melted

and driped on my shorts faster than I could eat it. [3] Even though it was unusualy hot, we started

to bike to the town pool. [4] Suddenly we heard sirens, so I slammed on my brakes and skided in

the dust. [5] Three firetrucks went raceing by. [6] My friend cryed out, "Look at the flames!"

[7] Smoke was begining to appear above the trees. [8] Worryed about our safety, we stood far

from the edge of the forest. [9] During Fire Prevention Week at school, we learnned that hot, dry

weather makes forest fires more likely. [10] The fire was put out, but a firefighter later said,

"Somebody was careless with a campfire, so the trees and animals payed the price."

PLURALS OF NOUNS I

16j   Form the plurals of most nouns by adding -s.

SINGULAR   duck   plate   mask   turkey   area   ruler

  PLURAL   ducks   plates   masks   turkeys   areas   rulers

16k   Form the plurals of nouns ending in *s, x, z, ch,* or *sh* by adding -es.

SINGULAR   brush   class   duplex   leash   watch

  PLURAL   brushes   classes   duplexes   leashes   watches

NOTE   Proper nouns usually follow this rule, too.

EXAMPLES   the Curtises   the Sánchezes
             the Thomases   the Katzes

EXERCISE 9   Spelling the Plurals of Nouns

On the line after each noun, write its correct plural form.

EX. tax   <u>taxes</u>

1. dish   _____
2. pillow   _____
3. reflex   _____
4. Pérez   _____
5. ranch   _____
6. wish   _____
7. field   _____
8. monkey   _____
9. guess   _____
10. closet _____
11. bench   _____
12. flash   _____
13. Martínez _____

14. ax   _____
15. dance   _____
16. idea   _____
17. chimney _____
18. harness _____
19. Jones   _____
20. dash   _____
21. candle   _____
22. kiss   _____
23. waltz   _____
24. rocket   _____
25. stitch   _____

16l **Form the plurals of nouns ending in _y_ preceded by a consonant by changing the _y_ to _i_ and adding _-es_.**

SINGULAR   baby   cherry   daisy   lily   surgery
  PLURAL   bab**ies**   cherr**ies**   dais**ies**   lil**ies**   surger**ies**

EXCEPTION   With proper nouns, simply add _-s_.
                    EXAMPLES   the Barkleys, the Murphy**s**

16m **Form the plurals of nouns ending in _y_ preceded by a vowel by adding _-s_.**

SINGULAR   bay   valley   Monday   toy   guy
PLURAL   bay**s**   valley**s**   Monday**s**   toy**s**   guy**s**

16n **Form the plurals of most nouns ending in _f_ by adding _–s_. The plurals of some nouns ending in _f_ or _fe_ are formed by changing the _f_ to _v_ and adding either _–s_ or _–es_.**

SINGULAR   reef   chief   life   shelf   leaf   gulf
  PLURAL   reef**s**   chief**s**   li**ves**   shel**ves**   lea**ves**   gulf**s**

NOTE   When you are not sure how to spell the plural of a noun ending in _f_ or _fe_, look in a dictionary.

16o **Form the plural of compound nouns consisting of a noun plus a modifier by making the modified noun plural.**

SINGULAR   sister-in-law   sea horse   Chief of State
  PLURAL   sister**s**-in-law   sea horse**s**   Chief**s** of State

EXERCISE 10   _Spelling the Plurals of Nouns_

On the line after each noun below, write its correct plural form.

EX.   company   <u>companies</u>

1. pen pal   _____
2. library   _____
3. handkerchief   _____
4. mystery   _____
5. wife   _____
6. coat-of-arms   _____
7. victory   _____
8. scarf   _____
9. staff   _____
10. subway   _____

11. country   _____
12. Brodsky   _____
13. journey   _____
14. melody   _____
15. goal post   _____
16. half   _____
17. boy   _____
18. Sunday   _____
19. galaxy   _____
20. elf   _____

PLURALS OF NOUNS II

16p Form the plurals of nouns ending in *o* preceded by a vowel by adding -*s*. The plurals of many nouns ending in *o* preceded by a consonant are formed by adding -*es*.

SINGULAR	radio	studio	echo	potato
PLURAL	radios	studios	echoes	potatoes

EXCEPTIONS	tuxedo	hello
PLURAL	tuxedos	hellos

Form the plurals of most musical terms ending in *o* by adding -*s*.

SINGULAR	cello	tango	piccolo	piano
PLURAL	cellos	tangos	piccolos	pianos

NOTE   To form the plurals of some nouns ending in *o* preceded by a consonant, you may add either -*s* or -*es*.

SINGULAR	volcano	cargo	tornado
PLURAL	volcanos	cargos	tornados
	or	or	or
	volcanoes	cargoes	tornadoes

16q   The plurals of a few nouns are formed in irregular ways.

SINGULAR	woman	goose	child	mouse	fish
PLURAL	women	geese	children	mice	**fish**

EXERCISE 11   Spelling the Plurals of Nouns

On the line after each noun, write its correct plural form. Use a dictionary as needed.

EX.   tomato   <u>tomatoes</u>

1. zoo _____
2. zero _____
3. alto _____
4. ox _____
5. foot _____

6. deer _____
7. motto _____
8. trio _____
9. tooth _____
10. patio _____

EXERCISE 12   Identifying Incorrect Spelling in a Paragraph

The paragraph below contains several errors in spelling. Underline the incorrect words. Write the correct spelling above each misspelled word. If the sentence has no errors, write *C* above the sentence. [Hint: One sentence contains two errors.]

EX.   Our entire family, both men and <u>woman</u>, have always liked music.
                women

[1] When my brother and I were young childs, we began enjoying music. [2] We had radioes in our rooms, and we would tune in whenever we could. [3] I enjoyed pianoes more than any other instrument. [4] My brother liked to listen to stringed instruments, like celloes and banjoes. [5] Our father preferred to hear the high notes of the flutes and piccoloes. [6] For my mother, the sound of drums was the best, and drummers were her heros. [7] Our grandparents, on the other hand, listened to operas every chance they could. [8] At any time of the day, the family loved to hear musical echos throughout the house. [9] Now, whenever there are family gatherings on holidaies, we have some kind of music and song. [10] Everyone joins in, sopranoes and tenors alike.

MODULE REVIEW

A. Correcting Spelling Errors in Sentences

Underline the misspelled word in each sentence below. Then write the misspelled word correctly on the line before the sentence.

EX. __their__   Bicycle riders used to push against the ground with <u>thier</u> feet.

_____ 1. Bicycles today look very different from models that preceeded them.

_____ 2. The front wheels of some early bicycles were largeer than the rear wheels.

_____ 3. On one model, the hieght of the wheel was five feet.

_____ 4. Obviously, a rider could not climb on the seat easly.

_____ 5. Many riders had to have stitchies as the result of falls.

_____ 6. Nonetheless, these bicycles were a familiar sight along the highwayes in the 1870s.

_____ 7. One turn of the pedal would move the bicycle forward an amazeing distance.

_____ 8. As the front wheels became smaller, bicycles became safer for adults and childs.

_____ 9. Instead of siting on top of the large wheel, a rider could sit between the wheels.

_____ 10. Still, the rider had to watch out for wet, slippery leafs on the sidewalk.

B. Proofreading a Paragraph to Correct Spelling Errors

The following paragraph contains twenty spelling errors. For each sentence, underline the misspelled word or words. Write the correct spelling above each misspelled word.

living

EX. A coral reef is home to many <u>liveing</u> creatures.

[1] Many mysteryous creatures live on beautyful coral reeves. [2] Sponges come in

many shapes and sizes and are sometimes the color of lemmons or potatos. [3] Provideing homes for small creatures, they anchor themselfs to rocks or other objects under the water.

[4] These creatures get food from the water that passes through the sponges' bodys. [5] Coral reefs are formed by skeletons of billions of tiney animals caled coral polyps. [6] One sea animal you may find there will not be noticable. [7] For example, octopuss can change color to match their surroundings. [8] Most of these animales measure only several inchs in length.

[9] Because they are bonless, they can easyly squeeze through small openings. [10] To confuse their enemys, they shoot out inky liquid and then hastyly procede to safety.